# STRONGER THAN YOU THINK

# KERRY EVANS

## WITH KATIE WHYATT

# STRONGER THAN YOU THINK

## THE AUTOBIOGRAPHY

### FOREWORD BY RYAN REYNOLDS
### AFTERWORD BY ROB McELHENNEY

\Bᵇ\

**Biteback Publishing**

First published in Great Britain in 2025 by
Biteback Publishing Ltd, London
Copyright © Kerry Evans 2025

ISBN 978-1-83736-017-8

10 9 8 7 6 5 4 3 2 1

A CIP catalogue record for this book is available from the British Library.

Set in Minion Pro

Printed and bound in Great Britain by
CPI Group (UK) Ltd, Croydon CR0 4YY

FSC
www.fsc.org
MIX
Paper | Supporting
responsible forestry
FSC® C013604

*Nan, you were literally my world.*
*I simply adored you.*
*I wish you were here to read this – you'd have read it in a day!*
*Love you always xx*

# CONTENTS

# FOREWORD
## *BY RYAN REYNOLDS*

I've been asked to write a foreword. I assumed that meant, like, a paragraph. Maybe less? A brief statement or simple grunt. But then I was told the story was Kerry Evans's – and suddenly, just a paragraph felt like a bit of a d*ck move. I'm sure she asked Rob first. But everybody knows Rob likes to draw pictures. In crayon. Which makes his worth in the exciting and delicate medium of a foreword useless as f*ck.

So here I am. Vulnerable, inspired… unpaid. And perhaps worst of all, outmatched by the courage, humour and soul of the woman you're about to meet.

Let's start at the beginning. Not Kerry's beginning – you'll get to that in Chapter One. I'm talking about the other beginning. The moment two Hollywood schmucks showed up at Wrexham AFC. (Not naming names, but only one half of this partnership actually LIVES IN HOLLYWOOD. Because of my devotion, I've been living at the stadium for the better part of a year. Only Chal knows. And the player that shall remain nameless – you know who you are – who brings me Nando's every Thursday.)

Where were we? Ah! Yes. The other beginning. The schmucks

inevitably came a-knockin' on Wrexham's door. Just like the prophets foretold. The prophets, in this case, being me and Rob McElhenney. (Note to reader: Rob's last name can – at times – be tricky. We all call him 'Rob Mac'. But on *Welcome to Wrexham*, it's McElhenney.)

As we secretly sashayed our way through the town and its inhabitants, we soon met a disarmingly candid Welshman named Spencer Harris: part-time martial artist and full-time wonderful husband, father and friend.

And then he picked up the phone to someone with whom we'd later share the unlikeliest of phone calls. 'Kerry, we've had a request,' Spencer began. 'Ryan Reynolds and Rob McElhenney want to speak to you.'

Now imagine you're Kerry Evans. You've lived through enough drama to fill ten biopics and a 348-episode order of *Coronation Street*. You've battled systemic apathy, endured eye-watering physical trauma that only a woman of peerless mental discipline could withstand and yet still found a way to give other disabled Wrexham fans the opportunity to attend away games. In short, Kerry's story doesn't need a Canadian movie star and an American pantomime showing up to make things feel any more cinematic. And yet… hi!

When Rob and I first heard Kerry's name, it came with the canonised respect reserved for saints, superheroes or Canada's official moustache, Robert Goulet. 'You need Kerry onside,' someone told us. It sounded strategic. But what they really meant was: you boneheads need Kerry to remind you what the hell this is all for.

So we called Kerry. We Zoomed over a thousand Wrexham fan owners. We tried our best to seem chill. Rob probably rehearsed for days, possibly weeks, before these meetings. To project power and intelligence, I wore a jet-black turtleneck I'd stolen from Spencer Harris's bedroom when I got 'lost' looking *pour le toilette*.

Turtlenecks make no sense. It's like having your torso attacked by Steve Jobs if he was made of molten hot lava.

But when Rob spoke to Kerry? Kerry was calm. Curious. Controlled. She asked questions. She listened. And when Rob said: 'Would you like to come on a journey with us?' he sensed the flicker in her eyes. Not just of hope, but of someone who'd spent a lifetime hauling coal out of dark mines and crushing it into diamonds. She knew, instinctively, a door had creaked open. A door of opportunity for those that opportunity had, effectively and openly, excluded.

Kerry won't say anything remotely close to self-aggrandisement. But it isn't aggrandisement if it's a simple, elegant truth: she was already the soul of Wrexham long before we ever showed up.

This book is the story of that soul. And while I'm tempted to describe it as 'inspirational', that word feels too small, too polished and trite. Like a label you slap on a quote above a beach photo. Plus, I don't know how to read.

Kerry's story isn't inspiration. It's ignition. It lights something inside yourself – a belief that no matter what your body does or what the world says, you can manifest the impossible. You can build systems of kindness, connection, impact and togetherness.

Kerry never set out to be famous. All she ever wanted was to help one person. Just one. The irony, of course, is that she's helped hundreds, if not thousands. Probably you, by the time you reach the end of this book.

Football is at its best when it transcends the sport and reveals something bigger. And for me, that something is 'togetherness'. When people walk into the STōK Cae Ras, they check their identity politics at the door. They're wearing the same shirts, waving the same colours and they sing and chant the same songs. It's one of the few spaces we have left where we come together with no intention of hurting each other. Just winning. Or drawing. Or losing with some grace. It is far and away my favourite place on earth. It's my *Field of Dreams.*

Wisdom like Kerry's is a hard-fought prize. Earned by her willingness to engage in a moment-by-moment showdown with herself. And Kerry has transcended what it means to make spaces inclusive. She's also made space for the one person she wasn't expecting: herself.

In this book, you'll read about a girl who, when shoved by pain, shoved back. A mother who weathered storms, too many to count. A volunteer who became a changemaker. A Wrexham supporter who found, in football, the thing she'd always given others: belonging. And that, at least to me, is the essence and the perfection of the beautiful game.

It's time I hand the mic over to Kerry. Read this slowly. Absorb each page. Because while *Welcome to Wrexham* may have introduced the world to this football club, this book will introduce the world to its heart. Her name is Kerry Evans.

*Ryan Reynolds*
*Wrexham AFC Co-Owner*
*Unlicensed Blanket Folder*
*Very Lucky Human*

# PROLOGUE

'We've had a request,' begins Spencer Harris, the director of Wrexham AFC. It's 7 November 2020. I'm in the lounge, watching early evening TV.

I remember the date because what happens a few days later – who calls me, and where they call from – will be so extraordinary that I'll mark the moment with a Facebook post. It will amount to no more than one line in the sea of words written about Wrexham AFC amid one of the most extraordinary takeovers in world sport. But I don't know that at the time. I don't know of all that is to come: the Emmy award-winning TV show, the international headlines, the Hollywood superstars that we will welcome to our club. I don't know of the effect that it will have on me, a voluntary disability liaison officer with cerebral palsy who is weeks away from working for one of the biggest names in the film industry and a very successful American TV star.

I sit in shock, listening intently as Spencer continues. 'Ryan Reynolds and Rob McElhenney want to speak to you. Am I OK to give them your phone number?'

I pause, lower the phone from my ear. 'Well, yes,' I stutter. 'Yes, of course.'

These are the moments I look back on, over four years into our football fairy tale, when I wonder how we got here. How I, little old Kerry who began volunteering at Wrexham in 2016, became swept up in all of this. How a non-league football club in an unglamorous area of North Wales, which survived for years only on the generosity of its fans, became the luckiest team in the world.

£12 a year. That was how much it cost to be a Wrexham owner in 2020, and there were more than a thousand of us. Together, we made up the Wrexham Supporters Trust (WST). No matter how much money you put in – the equivalent of £1 a month, as I did, or £1,000 a year – everyone had the same say. Nobody was more of an owner than anybody else and, crucially, each of us had a voice.

Aside from managers and players, the club employed just a few full-time members of staff: the groundsman, stadium manager, commercial manager, shop and ticketing staff, club secretary and head of youth. Everyone else had full-time jobs elsewhere and ran the football club as volunteers.

There was the six-person Wrexham AFC Board of Directors, comprising fans overseeing all the day-to-day logistics. They looked after the money, sorted the deals for new players and held all the secrets. They answered to the Wrexham AFC Supporters Trust Board: twelve elected fans who acted on behalf of all fan owners. Spencer Harris, a strategic director at Kellogg's, was the public face of the club and the one who would put his head above the parapet. We didn't have a full-time CEO; the role was divided between the directors, all unpaid. We held ownership meetings quarterly to discuss the direction of the club.

Wrexham was almost an after-work hobby. We held meetings in

the evenings and sorted out the odds and ends at weekends. That was how the club ran for twelve years.

At the time, I was a big fan of our model of fan ownership. I thought it was incredible. Here we were, still a big, identifiable club throughout North Wales, even in the National League, doing it on our own in the spare time people grabbed between work and family and life. Volunteers were running the football club out of duty and passion. I really respected that. Ultimately, it was why I joined. It was why I built my own role up from a part-time one to the equivalent of a full-time job, without earning a penny.

But the model had its drawbacks. It's only now, with the benefit of hindsight and Hollywood money, that I've realised how limited we were. There was never enough money in the pot, so the same story kept repeating itself: the minute we had a special player, we had to sell them because we needed money to run the club. We also had to pay what those in the boardroom call 'the National League premium' – that little bit extra to encourage players to drop out of the English Football League.

On top of that, the National League (the fifth tier of English football) is a tricky division to get out of, in part because there's only one automatic promotion spot (League Two has three, and League One and the Championship have two). In 2011, a haul of ninety-eight points – then a record for the club – wasn't enough to get us promoted automatically. Increasingly, we found ourselves coming up against clubs with rich owners and bigger budgets. In 2013, we were beaten in the play-offs by Newport County, bankrolled by a former mechanic who had won the Euromillions. Salford City had won promotion in 2019 funded by Manchester United's Class of '92.

We knew that we could never go out and buy the top striker or the best players, and a divide was building between those who were wary of welcoming new owners at the expense of losing fan control of the club and those who thought it was time to try something different.

During the pandemic, the stakes were higher still. Put simply, we didn't know where the money was going to come from without supporters coming through the turnstiles or sponsors paying for the advertising hoardings. First team players were furloughed and had to take on extra work, in supermarkets or as delivery drivers, to support their families. On the field, the curtailed 2019/20 season ended with the club's lowest result in 156 years when Wrexham finished twentieth in the National League.

Most nights, I went to bed filled with anxiety over the future of the club. I knew the players and their families. What would happen to them if they lost their jobs? What would happen to us without Wrexham? I still received my state benefits throughout the pandemic, but my work was never about money for me.

Wrexham AFC saved my life. I don't mean that I would have died had the club not come into my life, but it found me at a time when I didn't know what my purpose was. After a cerebral bleed that could have killed me in September 2005 but instead left me in a wheelchair and without feeling down my right side, I'd left the workplace and woke up every day in pain and with no reason to get out of bed. I didn't have an identity or know what to do with each day. I never thought I'd work again. That bubbly Kerry who had always refused to let her cerebral palsy hold her back felt like a distant memory. I was a shell of myself again, back to being that lonely teenager who never thought she'd be accepted or make anything of her life.

Wrexham brought the world to me. That's how it saved me.

Take my 2018 fundraising to put on accessible away travel for wheelchair users. I sold red blankets emblazoned with the club crest to raise the £3,500 we needed to cover several away fixtures that season. My husband Kings and I had ordered 680 blankets, each individually wrapped, and spent our evenings in the living room unpacking and repackaging them all: the club's kit suppliers, Macron, had offered to embroider Wrexham's crest at a cut price if Kings and I took care of all the packaging for them. At the first fixture we offered our accessible travel to, against Solihull Moors, grown men were in tears because they'd never been to an away match before. En route to a London fixture, we met up with other coaches of fans at a service station, and when everyone started chanting together, I knew it had all been worth it.

Those interactions are what keep me at Wrexham: the families I meet and the impact I have on them. I'm proud that I'm good at the work I do there. I'm proud that, every day, I do things I never thought I'd be able to. And I'm proud of the effect my efforts have on the club's supporters.

I owe a lot to Wrexham. That club is everything to me. And it could have gone under were it not for the discussions taking place in the background – discussions with two Hollywood superstars on the other side of the Atlantic.

There had been twelve approaches to buy Wrexham in the eleven years since the club went into the hands of the Wrexham Supporters Trust. We heard all the rumours – businesspeople, conmen, entrepreneurs, opportunists – but nothing ever came of them. If the interest had been serious, the WST would have put in place NDAs and the prospective buyer would have had to put up a bond of £5,000. That protected us from chancers and scared off the pretenders. As far as we knew, no NDA was ever signed in all that time.

This time was different. The rumours began: an offer had come in for the football club. A serious offer – so serious that it was being discussed among the board members. Every day, there were whispers, mutterings. I pulled aside somebody in the know and spoke to him off the record. The gist? 'This is big.'

As far as names went, though, the rumour mill was as silent as silent can be and I was none the wiser. Until I got the phone call. I was in the kitchen, preparing our tea, when the phone buzzed. It was someone else inside the club.

'Do you want to know the name?'

My heart stuttered. My voice hitched. 'I'd love to,' I began. 'But I know I'm not supposed to.'

For a second, I doubted whether I truly wanted to know. With a fan-owned club, everyone had big mouths and loose lips. People knew everything, even if they weren't supposed to. And there was leak after leak after leak. I've never, to this day, disclosed anything confidential to journalists or on social media. But at a small club, you're always under suspicion. 'You were there. You were in that meeting,' they'll say, or 'I told you this – who else did you tell?'

*Did I want to know?* My mind toyed with itself. Say I found out. If those names ever got out prematurely, the club could turn around and point the finger at me. I knew I wouldn't go to the press, but I didn't want the blame thrown my way if somebody else did.

I paused, suspended in that breath between knowing and not knowing. *Once I find out,* I thought, *there will be no going back.*

'No, don't tell me,' I said. Then I changed my mind again. 'No. Go on.'

'Have you… have you ever heard of Ryan Reynolds?'

'Not on your life!' I shouted. 'Ryan Reynolds, going to buy Wrexham AFC?'

'It's true!' they protested. 'He wants to buy Wrexham – with Rob

McElhenney, from *Always Sunny*.' I turned to Kings, my husband. He nodded: he'd watched Rob's show, *It's Always Sunny in Philadelphia*, about a run-down Irish bar in the US.

'You're having us on.'

'I'm not, Kerry,' they insisted. 'Think about it. Where would I have dreamt that name up from if it wasn't true?'

They had a point. If you're winding somebody up, you're not going to come out with Ryan Reynolds buying Wrexham, are you? You'd aim your sights a little bit lower. My mind scuttled through all the other names we'd heard over the past few weeks. Robbie Savage had come up a lot. He had been born in Wrexham and played locally before joining Manchester United as a trainee once he finished school. Back when he was a player, he'd talked about the possibility of ending his career at Wrexham or one day managing the club. Russell Crowe came up, too, because his great-grandparents, Fred and Kezia Crowe, had run a fruit and vegetable wholesale business from Wrexham. Social media had declared Crowe a dead cert. I'd never seen *Gladiator*, but that would have been exciting enough.

This?

Kings and I spent the rest of the night laughing at each other in disbelief. The news didn't sink in because it was just too silly. How could we believe it? Why would Ryan Reynolds and Rob McElhenney buy a football club in Wrexham? A rich businessman would have been one thing, but even that would be nothing like whatever this was.

I was desperate to tell people, but that information never went any further than Kings, who always knows what's happening, and my dad, because he doesn't have social media and I trust him completely. If I'd been in that insider's position, I wouldn't have breathed a word.

It meant that Kings and I had to carry on with day-to-day life for the next few weeks, burying the secret. We spent half that time looking at each other in disbelief. *No, it can't be. It really can't be.* Every so often, we had to stop what we were doing and allow the thought to flash through our minds: *Ryan Reynolds.*

In late September, the names were made public. At an emergency meeting on 22 November, the WST voted to allow sale talks to go ahead with people they'd only known as 'two extremely well-known individuals of high net worth'. The day after, the club released the names.

Fans reacted exactly as we did: *Don't be so silly. This is a wind-up. It can't possibly be true.* Everyone knew Ryan Reynolds, but my daughter, Casey, was a far bigger fan of him than I was. 'This is wasted on you because you don't realise just how big this guy is,' she said to me.

Disbelief was on the faces of everyone volunteering at the club. It was the conversation on everybody's lips: 'We're going to work for Ryan Reynolds.'

And we quickly got a taste of what that would involve. We were told very early on that we wouldn't be allowed to speak to reporters without express permission from the media team. But they quickly became overwhelmed. Overnight, the car park teemed with press. For the next few weeks, camera crews snaked around the stands and reporters doorstepped us as we came and went each day from Wrexham's grounds, the Racecourse (now the Cae Ras). Journalists raced between the football club and The Turf, the pub next door, which would end up world famous thanks to *Welcome to Wrexham*. Wayne Jones, owner of The Turf, set up a butty van outside during the pandemic, and he and his customers became a goldmine for interviews. I'd often be stopped by a broadcaster asking for directions. 'We want to speak to Wayne,' they'd say, hopefully, their film crews hovering behind them.

I was at the club most days but wasn't based there because the offices, at that point, weren't wheelchair accessible. Still, my phone rang constantly with requests from our press officer: 'Can you come down and speak to ITV?' Then: 'Can you come down and speak to the BBC?'

I ended up being their go-to interviewee. As soon as one interview wrapped up, the camera crew from another television channel would be setting up in the background for my next one. 'What do you think of the takeover? Can we get your thoughts?'

Even at that point, I never imagined how global the Wrexham story would become and how fascinated the world would be with our little football club. Wrexham was home to a very working-class, unassuming community – one that never quite recovered economically from the closure of the pit and steelworks. Pound shops, charity shops and empty storefronts dominated the town centre. There was little investment, few jobs and a population growing frustrated at a lack of prospects. Redevelopment plans seemed to drag on for years and never amount to anything.

But the Wrexham people are very proud of our culture of sticking together. And that culture has been forged, in part, because of the football club.

Many fans were on edge at the talk of new owners. Given all that had happened in the past, they had good reason to be wary. Alex Hamilton, a former lawyer, had arrived in 2000 with his eyes fixed on the Racecourse. At that time, the stadium was owned by Marston's Brewery and leased to the club. Hamilton arranged for the club to buy the grounds – and hold it 'in trust' for his own company, Crucialmove. He had opened discussions with B&Q and wanted to sell the stadium and the land around it for commercial development.

By the time Wrexham supporters had driven out Hamilton, the Inland Revenue (now HMRC) had lodged a winding-up petition against the club. It had debts of £4 million, with over £880,000 in unpaid taxes. The remaining directors placed the club in financial administration in December 2004, and as a result Wrexham received a ten-point deduction from the Football League. We were the first league club ever to be penalised under the new rule. The club won its case to keep the Racecourse Ground, though.

The ripples spread outward for years. Wrexham was relegated to non-league football in 2008 after eighty-seven years in the league. Still, there were more difficulties to endure.

Ahead of the 2011/12 season, the Conference League demanded that the club pay a bond of £250,000 or face expulsion from the Blue Square Premier League (now the National League). By Monday 10 August, hours before the payment deadline, Wrexham still owed £100,000. The Red Passion Wrexham message board challenged fans to help the club find the money before 5.30 p.m.

People arrived at the club willing to donate their house deeds. Little kids came with their pocket money. People gave what they could. If you had a spare fiver, you handed it over. It galvanised the town, the fans rallying round with a single-minded focus: let's keep our club. And by 2.30 p.m., they'd found the money. Everyone says the same thing about their football club, but there really is just something about Wrexham fans. How do they do it, again and again and again? How do they keep defying the odds?

Within three months, the Wrexham Supporters Trust had gone further, and managed to fund the club's takeover. By asking fans like me to pay at least £12 a year to support their efforts, they had recruited almost 2,000 supporters in time to purchase the club at the end of November.

When the pandemic hit, there was a growing feeling that a rich owner might be the only way forward. That view was met with trepidation because nobody at Wrexham has a short memory. We remembered what had happened a decade earlier – and how quickly our club had been sold down the river. But Covid was destroying the club financially.

Ryan Reynolds and Rob McElhenney were our only hope.

• • • •

It wasn't out of the ordinary for Spencer Harris to call me.

'I've got a bit of a strange request for you, Kerry.'

'All right.' In my voluntary role, I was used to strange requests. I was endlessly fundraising, begging and borrowing to find the money we needed to make the club accessible for as many fans as possible.

'Ryan Reynolds and Rob McElhenney want to speak to you,' Spencer says. 'Am I OK to give them your phone number? I wasn't going to do it without asking.'

'Well, yes,' I stuttered. 'Yes, of course.' I was aghast. I couldn't say no, but I didn't get it – why would they want to speak with *me*?

'It won't be somebody calling on their behalf,' Spencer continued. 'One of them will contact you to have a chat. And I don't know when they're going to ring you, but it will be soon.'

I turned to Kings. He had muted the television for me to take the call and noticed my stunned expression. 'That was a mad one,' I said. He watched, my hand shaking, as I dialled my dad. I had to share this with him.

'You'll never guess what,' I said. 'Spencer Harris has just called. He's passing on my number to Ryan or Rob.' I held the phone away from my ear as I heard Mum screaming.

'What?' gasped Dad. 'Why? What do they want with you? When are they going to ring you?'

It was arguably the most important question, and as the days passed with no call from the US, I kicked myself for not asking Spencer that very thing. Why hadn't I? It was so unlike me: if I needed to know something, I made sure I found out. Why had I been so quiet this time? This was the biggest thing to happen in the club's history, and I'd only gone and kept myself in the dark. But the shock of it all had made it hard to know what to say.

We waited. Every time my phone chirped, I'd jump slightly, then my heart would slow when I realised it wasn't them. I spent my days in apprehension and suspense, planning and rehearsing what I'd say to them. But there was only so much preparation I could do when the one thing Spencer hadn't said was why they even wanted to speak to me. I replayed the conversation over and over in my mind, trying to remember exactly what he'd said: Ryan or Rob have asked if they can contact you. What did that even mean?

We waited. I didn't tell anyone at the club that I was waiting for a call. All I knew was that no other volunteers had spoken to our prospective owners.

Still we waited. Every day, Mum rang. 'Have you heard anything?'

'No, I haven't. And you don't need to ask! The minute I do, I'll call you.'

The more time went on, the more I wondered if they weren't going to phone after all. Perhaps they just didn't need to speak to me any-more. Maybe they'd never needed to in the first place and someone had made a mistake. After all, I was only the voluntary disability liaison officer – I didn't hold all the purse strings. And Spencer had been short on the specifics. All I could do was wait for my phone to light up with what I assumed would be a withheld number.

Late one evening. I finally heard from them. I wheeled myself into the lounge as Kings flicked through the channels on the TV. My phone buzzed.

I looked over at Kings. 'It… It says California on the phone,' I breathed.

'Get lost,' he chuckled.

'Kings – it says it right there.' I held the screen up to him, my hand shaking again.

'Well, you'd better answer it then, before he hangs up.'

I reversed, pulling through the lounge into the dining room.

'Hello?'

'Hey! Is that Kerry Evans?'

'Yes.'

'It's Rob McElhenney here.' An absurd thought struck me: *It's helpful that he said his name.* I wouldn't have known what either of them sounded like.

I swallowed, forcing out my reply. 'Thanks for ringing,' I managed. 'How are you?'

'I'm good. It's so good to speak to you.'

*Your voice is shaking!* I snapped at myself. I could feel my throat closing up. In all my imaginings of this call, all my thousands of rehearsals and practice runs, I'd never been this nervous. I never thought I'd sound so stupid. I looked over my shoulder to see Kings loitering in the archway, craning his neck to hear.

Rob explained that he'd spoken to Wrexham's board about the important people he and Ryan needed to get onside before the take-over. In response, the board had given him two names. The first was

Dixie McNeil, the Wrexham legend who became club president in 2013. The second was mine. My name, he said, had come up again and again. He used the word 'unanimously'.

'I hope you don't mind me calling,' he said. 'Spencer Harris gave me your number.'

'Of course.'

'You're obviously aware we want to buy Wrexham.'

'Yes.'

Rob knew a lot about me and what I'd created at the club. He knew of the fundraising I'd done to put on accessible away travel for wheelchair users. He knew about how I'd turned a derelict old kiosk, used as an unofficial storeroom, into a sensory room to make our stadium an autism-friendly environment. He knew how, as a volunteer, I'd brought the club in line with the accessibility standards set for higher division clubs. He knew that I was looking to set up a powerchair football team for wheelchair users. He and Ryan had clearly done their homework, whether aided by the board or Google.

'You've done absolutely fantastic things for the club regarding disability,' he said. He was so down-to-earth that it felt as though I'd spoken to him before: he felt familiar, somehow, even though I'd never seen *Always Sunny*. I felt calm, at ease. This was the most extraordinary phone call of my life, but it felt so… normal.

'Thank you very much,' I said. 'I love what I'm doing. It's an absolute honour to do the job that I do.'

It was true. I could see the impact that my work had on the lives of our supporters, and that always made me want to do more. I thought of the dad who'd only ever been able to take one of his twins to Wrexham matches because the other had autism and couldn't cope. Our Quiet Zone had meant that they could all go together.

The dad had been in tears as he told me: 'I don't think you realise how big it is for me to bring both of my boys to the football.'

'I can't believe you did all that as a volunteer,' Rob continued.

'It wasn't easy, but being given the opportunity by Wrexham was enormous to me,' I explained. 'I didn't ever think that I could achieve what I have.'

'We're going to back you up with anything you want,' he said. 'We'll back you all the way.'

My mind raced with the possibilities. Everything I'd delivered at Wrexham to that point had been done on a shoestring. I thought of the quiz nights I'd held, the raffles I'd run, the locals I'd asked to chip in out of the goodness of their hearts, all to scrape together the money we needed. 'Yes, you can do it, Kerry,' the board would tell me whenever I came to them with my latest idea, 'but you'll have to sort the funds.'

Someone coming in with Hollywood money would change everything. It hit me: we would be able to move mountains with this kind of backing.

Rob explained that he and Ryan were holding a Zoom call with all the fan owners the following evening. He wanted to mention in the meeting that we had spoken and that they were fully behind the amazing job I'd done. He asked my permission to do so.

'Yes, of course,' I said. 'I'm an owner. I'll be on that call.'

'Well, we'll see you tomorrow night,' he said. 'Ryan and I are very excited about getting our story out to the fans. Hopefully, it will go our way and we'll end up buying Wrexham AFC. So,' he paused, 'are you up for coming on this journey with us?'

My hand shook as I tapped out an update to Facebook: 'It's not every day you get a call from Rob McElhenney from Hollywood.'

# CHAPTER ONE

# MUM KNOWS BEST

This is the story my parents have told me about my birth for as long as I can remember.

My mum, Susan Jones, was admitted to hospital to be induced when I was a week overdue. She had just one contraction, and after several hours, the hospital staff concluded that I was not ready to be born. They sent her home for one more week.

On 5 August 1975, she entered the hospital again for a second try. Anticipating a long labour, they gave her an epidural and hooked her up to a machine to register my heartbeat. They sent my dad over to the pub across the road, probably with instructions to take his time. The nurses' view was that nothing would happen quickly.

Mum was in no pain but watched as the machine flashed and beeped.

'It looks as if she's in distress,' she said, concerned.

'That machine is always playing up,' replied the nurse, resetting it. 'She's absolutely fine. Don't worry. Take no notice of it. We can hear the heartbeat.'

Soon, it was all systems go. I was born before midnight, a forceps delivery with the cord wrapped twice around my neck but

1

otherwise, to my parents' knowledge, a perfectly healthy baby. Doctors came the next day, took me down to the special care baby unit and later returned me without a word. Mum reflects now that this must have been the point at which they realised I had cerebral palsy. No one ever told her.

I sat up, rolled, crawled and walked on time. The only inkling that something was amiss was when I would press my right thumb into the palm of my hand and clench my fist so tightly that my knuckles would turn purple. I would pull my fist to my chest and my arm would spasm. It was a subconscious movement whenever I was concentrating, whether I was brushing my teeth, playing with blocks or focusing on the TV. My nan – my mum's mum – would run her hand over mine, feeling for the tightness of the muscles in my hand and wrist. She would massage my fingers with lotions and oils until my grip loosened.

When I was around a year old, Dad was taken ill with appendicitis. Mum sent for Doctor Graham from our local surgery. Dad's appendix had burst so an ambulance was called. Mum's recollection of that day is that the doctor spent more time with me than he did my dad. He played on the floor with me, asked me to walk and studied me as we waited for the ambulance to arrive. On my right leg, I walked on the ball of my foot. Days later, he contacted my parents and told them that he would like to refer me to a specialist consultant.

My parents were given no inkling, in the meeting at the hospital, that they would be receiving big news. My dad didn't even go in; he stayed in the waiting room. Mum went to meet the consultant with me sat on her knee.

'Well, she's got cerebral palsy, hasn't she?' said the doctor, matter-of-factly.

There was no build-up, no explanation for how they'd arrived at that conclusion, why they'd wanted me checked out or why they'd asked Mum to bring me there. Mum was hurt that the doctor said this to her as though she'd always been aware, and she wondered later whether 'cerebral palsy' had been written in my medical record since birth. She didn't think to ask this on the day, however. Mum had never heard of cerebral palsy. She didn't know what they'd just labelled me with or what they were even talking about.

She says now that she is glad that she hadn't been told when I was just a few days old because she and my dad would have just panicked. As it was, she had been able to enjoy being in the baby bubble without worrying about what the future might hold.

In shock, she stood and took me, on autopilot, straight to have a brain scan. She has memories of me screaming and crying at the noise, the lights and the strangers sweeping in and out of the room – of trying to hold my head in place and soothe me. It was a traumatic day for her and she navigated it in a total daze, confused because she had already seen me walk. She had known I'd had an issue with my hand but hadn't realised that it hinted at anything like this.

Cerebral palsy is actually the name for a group of conditions affecting movement and coordination, and symptoms vary in their severity. Some struggle with speech, some have learning difficulties and others might be in a wheelchair from birth. Mum didn't know what the future held for me.

'Will she be able to dance?' Mum asked the consultant. She ran the Clifton School of Dance, and taught ballet, tap and modern.

'She'll never be able to coordinate easily or skip,' he replied. 'She may be able to go to a mainstream school, but it's too early to say. She might have to go to a special school.'

Mum says the doctor's next words were: 'Don't expect her to be able to do anything.' He told her that I'd never be able to 'do things other children can'. In the weeks and months afterwards, Mum thought back to the day of my birth and the machine flashing and beeping. She had been right: I was being starved of oxygen.

She was sent away with no leaflets or books. Support was scant. No one had the internet back then to find support groups or look things up. Mum and Dad didn't know how to access medical journals. All we had were annual visits to a specialist and Mum's confidence, as she watched me grow, that I would be able to attend a mainstream primary school. My speech was fine – I was so talkative, in fact, that on long car journeys my parents would actually pay me to see how long I could stay silent for.

Aged four, I had an operation to lengthen my Achilles tendon and help me walk more easily. I was unable to put my right foot flat on the floor or flex it, and as a result I'd walk on my toes. I left hospital in plaster, and later had a white plastic splint fitted. It slotted under the arch of my foot and onto my heel and climbed halfway up the back of my calf, fastened across the front with Velcro. My first pair of school shoes were one size too big so we could fit the splint into them. But the surgery didn't work well, and throughout my childhood I walked with a limp. The limp became more pronounced as I got older, although it wasn't noticeable until I grew tired. Then I'd trip up. I still have the ripple of the scar down my right leg from where they cut my Achilles and, even though I have no movement or feeling there now, sometimes it will flash purple when stretched or tight.

As I recovered from the surgery, we received a visit from an occupational therapist. Mum had been upset because she had watched me sitting in the window watching the other children play outside.

'She's missing being able to be out with the kids,' Mum said.

'I'll see what I can do,' said the occupational therapist, and they came back with a red wooden cart. The older kids in our cul-de-sac would call by with the words: 'Can we take Kerry out in the cart?' I would sit in it and they pulled me along by the handle. I can't say I *played* with them at that point, because I still couldn't climb out, but at least I was with them, out in the street and part of whatever they were doing.

I would see a specialist at his afternoon surgery at a special needs school nearby. I hated going because he stank of whisky. I remember sitting in his tiny waiting room with its three chairs facing the double doors into a gymnasium. The bell would ring and kids went past into the gym in wheelchairs and walking frames. I looked at them and felt lucky that I was able to walk. My cerebral palsy felt very removed from theirs. We used the same words for our conditions, but I would see this horrible man, then go away and come back in six or twelve months. I didn't need to be there every day.

There were ballet bars on the walls of his office, which also housed a patient bed, boxes with inflatable gym balls and a desk with a big leather chair. He would observe me as I walked up and down, checking my leg movement, getting me to rotate my hips and asking questions about my activity levels. There was never any focus on my hands.

Instead he would measure my legs. He always described my left leg as my 'good' leg and the right as my 'bad' one. They were significantly different lengths, and his plan was to operate when I turned eight. He would take some bone from my left leg and put it into my right, then do the same again when I turned eighteen. In the meantime, Mum was told to go to Clarks and get a built-up shoe for my right leg.

Mum considered this and wasn't sure how it would stop me from walking on my toes. She asked around and someone pointed her in the way of an osteopath. Mum had never heard of an osteopath but was willing to give it a shot, which was brave of her given she often felt like she just had to do whatever the doctors said. She had heard that things were in motion for my surgery, with the specialist keen to book an appointment to measure me up properly.

The osteopath practised in his house, with a separate door leading to an extension where he and his wife, also an osteopath, worked. From the desk beneath the window, he explained that I was displacing my right leg from the hip bone because of how I was walking.

Behind a screen was a bed fitted with a roll of white paper. The osteopath massaged up my spine with his fingers, remarking that he could feel the tightness stretching all the way to the middle of my spine. He worked by hand, then brought out the massage gun. The pressure increased incrementally, and by the end I was jerking away from him in discomfort. He brought out creams and oils and manipulated my spine and the hip joint.

For the final flourish, he shepherded me over to one side of the bed. I lay on my left side, facing the wall, with my right knee hanging over the bed, and he took my right knee into his hands. Using his elbow, he put his weight halfway down my right leg. CRACK! CRUNCH! The leg shifted back into the joint. As I got up, wincing, he stood behind me, pulled my legs up level with each other and withdrew a tape measure from his pocket.

'Yep!' he said. 'Absolutely spot on. Off you go.'

Mum rightly takes the credit for preventing me from having those unnecessary operations. The initial consultant had just measured my legs, observed that they were different lengths and never looked further to consider the reason: one leg wasn't sitting in the hip properly. I had never had the full range of movement in my right leg and my inability to put my heel down put pressure on my leg. Walking with a limp eventually knocked it out of place.

Mum could tell when I was desperate to have an appointment with the osteopath because I'd be in indescribable pain and walking fully on my tiptoes on my right leg. Most days, I didn't experience any pain due to my cerebral palsy, but I would feel the difference as time went on between treatments. The constant dull ache would transform into shooting pains into my hip joint that would grow more intense as the weeks went by. When the pain was at its worst, Mum would lie me on her bed and massage me with creams: through my hip joints, where my Achilles had been operated on and the tightest joints in my foot. My arm never brought me pain, but I couldn't cope with the weight of a saucepan or a heavy book.

We would pull into the osteopath's driveway and every step up the long, paved garden footpath would be a struggle. I'd come out again an hour later pain free. I could never walk perfectly, but I'd almost be able to put my foot flat. It would take months and months before my leg would get dislodged again and the pain would return. We couldn't see an osteopath on the NHS and I remember Mum and Dad saying that those visits were expensive, but they were always happy to pay because they knew the treatment worked.

Mum didn't tell the first specialist about the osteopath initially. At the appointment to measure me for the planned surgery, he stepped back from the bed in alarm.

'Well, I don't know what has happened here,' he said. 'I don't understand it. The last time I measured her legs they were different lengths. I'm measuring them again today and they're the same.'

Mum sat quietly, smirking away until she came out with the truth.

To, in my view, my parents' credit, they say now they never thought of me as a disabled child; I was just *their* child. Day to day, my parents refused to see what I couldn't do. It was almost like they refused to believe that I had cerebral palsy. I wonder if that is a generational thing, that they didn't want to admit that anything was wrong. They would urge me to do things like everybody else. 'You will be able to do it,' they'd say. 'Don't give up! You've got to keep going.'

That frustrated me sometimes. I remember thinking: *Why are they pushing me to do this? Why don't they realise how hard things can be?* But their attitude might also be why I never viewed myself as unable to keep up with other children. My parents were probably quite typical of the time in that they just wanted us all to get on with things. I've asked them since why they didn't sue the hospital or claim any benefits for me. 'We both had good jobs, so we wouldn't have dreamt of getting anything for you,' they explained.

It's true that they both had very good jobs and we never wanted for anything financially. Mum and Dad met working at Shotton Steelworks, just outside Chester. Mum finished to have me, and in time opened the Clifton School of Dance, Clifton being my dad's second name. Dad then got a job at Kemira Fertilisers and worked his way through the ranks. By the time he retired, he was purchasing manager.

That was a very, very high-powered job, so Mum was the primary caregiver while trying to run a dance school – one so successful that my younger brother Ian and I would regularly joke that we had to share her with 150 other kids.

When I was a baby, Mum took me to classes with her, and I sat up at the front and watched. Once I turned three and my friends from nursery joined, I started taking classes myself. Mum hoped that they would help with my coordination.

Mum would be out teaching until 9.30 p.m. and would be so tired in the morning that we would have to wake her up two or three times before she'd stir. She would start teaching again at 4 p.m. In the days before she passed her driving test, she would pick us up from school, with Ian in his pushchair and her dance kit swinging from the pram, and we'd walk to the Boys' Brigade Hall in Hope to get ready for classes. My dad, still in his work suit, would collect us at six and take us home, where Mum would have plated up our dinners and lined them on the counter like the porridge from Goldilocks and the Three Bears: Dad's, mine and Ian's. Dad would bath us and put us to bed before Mum got home.

Nan was the backbone of the dance school and helped to run Mum's business, organising the registers and liaising with parents while Mum did the teaching. Nan would stay until closing, and then go home to Chester, to Granddad. He spent every afternoon and evening watching sports on his own at home so that Nan could help Mum. Granddad was the kindest man you could ever wish to meet. He was so proud of his family and besotted with his grandchildren. My youngest brother, Matt, was born when I was thirteen, and like Ian, he joined my mum's dancing school. When my brothers were on stage, Granddad would spend the whole performance moving among the audience telling anyone who'd listen that the stars of the show were his grandsons.

Granddad, as it happened, had a brush with Hollywood far earlier than I did. He served in the Chindits, a guerilla army regiment in Burma during the Second World War. Year after year, he told the tale of his unit's white donkey. They took it in turns to walk the animal, which they had to cover in mud to help camouflage it. It was raining one day when it was Granddad's turn, but with the mud washed off he was an easy target for the Japanese sniper in the trees. He always maintained that the donkey saved his life by taking the worst of the fire, as well as the shrapnel that shot out after the creature's load exploded. Who airlifted him to hospital? None other than Jackie Coogan, a child star who acted alongside Charlie Chaplin in *The Kid* and later played Uncle Fester in *The Addams Family* TV show. While in hospital, Granddad was given a samurai sword in recognition of his bravery. He hid it under his mattress before he went for surgery, but when he returned, it had been stolen.

At weekends, Mum took her dancers to festivals and competitions. I would sometimes go along and play with them in the wings, admiring the costumes – nearly all of them made by Nan. She was an excellent seamstress, and she always had her sewing machine out on the table working on her next project of intricate beads and sequins on tulle. When Matt came along, Nan would set up a makeshift playpen at the back of whichever competition hall we were at, positioning the chairs so that she could watch the dancers while keeping Matt safe and entertained with his toys.

Dance became a full-time job for Ian after he left home at sixteen to go to a performing arts college. When we dropped him off to live in the attic room of a three-storey house, I sobbed as I saw a little hand shoot out of the dormer window and wave goodbye. I missed him so much. He didn't move home after that, instead stepping straight into a successful acting career. The work never dried up for him.

We never, ever argued as children and we did so much together. I was in awe of his extroverted nature and how we would end up with our house full of other kids because they all just wanted to follow him.

Because there were thirteen years between Matt and me, I'd practically moved out before he was five. But I loved sitting on the floor and playing with him in those early years, taking over from Mum to give her a break.

Every year on Boxing Day, Father Christmas came to our family party and brought us extra presents. Nan had a very old-fashioned costume that someone would put on, with black Wellington boots. In those days, my Auntie Nora used to wrap up a tube of toothpaste as a gift, but the twist was she'd wrapped it up in a £5 note. In later years, when the Boxing Day party moved to my aunt and uncle's, Father Christmas's look changed as a friend of the family borrowed a more professional Santa costume from the zoo where they worked. None of the kids ever queried the drastic transformation, but he suddenly turned from a man in an old hand-me-down red suit to the real deal.

Matt started to get cocky one year, sure that he knew which relative was behind the beard. Said relative would leave right before Father Christmas appeared and materialised right after he walked out. You could see the confusion on Matt's face as he struggled to work it out. This tradition continued well into the family's next generation, only stopping when Covid hit.

I took dance exams until I was about eight. By then, I'd started to struggle because of my disability. We have videos of old dancing shows and plays, including one in which I sat in a nightie and Ian in a pair of pyjamas with a little teddy while I sang 'I Saw Mommy Kissing Santa Claus'. The other kids in the production were dancing and I had the vocal part because I couldn't keep up. A lot of dance seemed to fly over my head, to be honest, but it was one of Ian's big passions. When Ian was competing, dancers from different schools would rush over to watch him, because he really was that good. Adjudicators would always say things like 'I really hope you're heading into a dancing career!' as they called him forward again for first place.

We spent the first six years of my life in a house in a cul-de-sac, my parents having picked the plot when the street was being built. Next door lived two older boys, Dave and Steve, whose mum, Little

Sue, worked in the Post Office on the street next to the secondary school. Steve was a few years older than me and my favourite. He was the one who'd collect me in the cart and take me out.

'If you let me take her, I'll look after her,' he'd tell my mum. She trusted him and we made so many happy memories with the other kids on our road. Even when he got into video games, he'd invite me over and we'd play together. He treated me nicely, showed me he cared, and I adored him.

We stayed friends even after my family moved house, and I adored Steve for years. He used to joke with me: 'I'll wait for you, Kerry! I will marry you!' We still laugh about it to this day. When my Christmas card from Steve and his wife, Nicky, arrives, I joke that it's my best present and that I'll sleep with it under my pillow until next year. Kings tells me that the other man is hiding in plain sight.

I wonder what younger Kerry would have thought if she knew that Steve would be the first person to send her flowers. She'd probably be less impressed to learn that Steve sent them because he had just run her over.

He was one of the first in our friendship group to pass his driving test. He wasn't driving particularly fast on the day he came around the bend leading to our secondary school at nine in the morning. My best friend Joanne and I were running across the road, but I, of course, was slower. Everyone else's version of events – which they all find hilarious – is that I froze as soon as I looked across and locked eyes with Steve. My version of events is that I didn't have a clue it was him, but I watched as his car missed Joanne and barrelled straight into me.

The headmaster scooped me up off the tarmac, carried me to a house over the road and laid me down while Steve ran into the Post Office in a panic: 'Mum! Mum! I've run over Kerry!'

That night, Steve called with a bouquet of flowers, an apology and a new school bag because mine had been shredded under his front wheel. But that wasn't the first time I'd been in an accident.

Back when we lived in the cul-de-sac, there were a few other kids aside from Steve and Dave next door: Annette, two Matthews, Rachael and Katie. Our street was a safe space until the day I got run over by a milk float.

Mum and Dad would never let me cross the road because of my limp. Even though being on a cul-de-sac meant that the only cars we saw belonged to people who lived with us, I was slower than the other kids and my mum was cautious, making me walk all the way to the bend and back down.

I was dutiful for years and years. The day I decided I'd had enough of all that, I watched as Annette emerged from behind a parked car and darted across the road. *Nobody will know*, I thought, as I saw Annette waiting on the other side. So I stepped off the kerb… just as a milk float was trundling up the road. I ended up on the floor with my legs underneath the engine because I hadn't seen it coming.

When the news reached my mum, she knew instantly what I'd been trying to do. She and the neighbours flooded the street in a panic. I had scrapes and bruises, but otherwise I was fine. My husband Kings thinks this is hilarious, because how can anyone get run over by anything as slow as a milk float? It could only happen to me. The slowest accident in Wrexham history.

• • •

When I was six, my parents moved us from our three-bedroom semi to one of the two four-bedroomed detached houses on the bend sweeping through the nearby estate.

Some twelve doors down – on the same side, so I didn't have to cross the road and get hit by anything – lived Joanne, who would become my best friend. Over the road from her house was my new primary school. Although she was twelve months younger than me, our years were combined into one class and soon we were thick as thieves. We balanced each other out quite well because I was a happy-go-lucky kid and Joanne was always very steady and calm. My younger brother Ian is twelve months older than Joanne's brother Steve and they, too, became very close.

Joanne shared a room with her sister Helen. During school holidays, we'd kick Helen out and she'd have to top and tail with Steve so that Joanne and I could have the twin beds. I'd always take Little Ted – a once-cream plush teddy who, after years of wear and tear, wore a suit knitted for him by Nan just to hold him together. I've had him since the day I was born.

'He stinks!' Joanne would say, throwing him out of her bedroom window into the back garden below. My bond with Little Ted has lasted, however; I still keep him by my bed to this day even though his fur is long gone.

Joanne and I shared one of my biggest childhood passions: horses. Every Saturday morning, my parents would buy me a pony magazine and I kept every copy neatly organised in a binder in my room. Afterwards, they would take me to a stable for an hour of riding lessons. Twelve of us would ride the horses in a ring, learning how to canter, making meagre jumps as our parents watched on.

'Would you like to go and look at a pony and see if you would like your own?' my parents asked on the most bizarre Sunday morning of my life. Even then, I had sense enough to find it strange: what kid doesn't even ask for a horse and ends up getting one? It sounded ridiculous. I wouldn't have even thought I'd be worthy of a horse.

I didn't know at the time that the pony was intended to replace the dancing and to help with my coordination; I did know scores of kids obsessed with horses whose parents refused to let them have one because owning one required too much care. My dad knew what he was getting into because he'd grown up on a farm. He had lost his mother when he was nine. As a result, he and my uncle had to grow up fast and took on lots of jobs feeding the animals before school in the morning. Years later, when he was grieving, Dad would sleepwalk. One right turn out of the house and he would have walked straight into the road, but they only ever found him in a barn nearby, asleep among the hay bales. I wonder if that suggests that, psychologically, the farm was some kind of safe space for him – but in any case, he was so comfortable with farm life that he used to ride horses bareback.

In my riding hat and boots, I went to look at a palomino called Bianco. Palomino horses are a very popular breed, with their golden coat and cream mane. I fell in love with her instantly.

She arrived the following weekend in a horse box. Our front windows looked out onto Hope Mountain, and we rented the first field for her so that I could watch her from the lounge window. Dad paid to have a joiner make a shelter for Bianco out of corrugated metal sheets and a wooden frame.

That pony became my life, although she wasn't always well behaved. She would have days where she didn't want to be caught. I would be a few inches away from her and she would make eye contact before darting off and stalling. We'd repeat this game until I was exhausted and ready to admit defeat, and I would trudge home disappointed that I hadn't been able to catch her. When I started going to pony club on a Sunday, we had to arrive at 10 a.m. to be scored on how our horses looked. I remember going one morning to get Bianco ready and discovering that she had rolled in every puddle going. Her beautiful cream coat had turned black. I shook my head in panic, knowing what it would take to get her ready.

Joanne loved Bianco and used to spend hours trying to persuade her mum to let her have a pony of her own. 'I've got three kids, and you all get equal,' came the reply. 'You're not having a horse!'

In the end, Joanne rented a pony from someone who had outgrown theirs and we would go out riding together. We entered gymkhanas and enrolled in summer schools. Joanne's grandparents lived on a farm in Minera, and we would visit them on weekends to play in the hay. Joanne's other nan visited every Thursday. She used to call me Teri even after she'd been corrected. 'I know it's Teri!' she'd say dismissively.

I outgrew Bianco after a few years, so we sold her locally. When Joanne and I went hacking to her new home, Bianco would bolt over at the sound of my voice. We kept that up for years and I loved that she'd stayed loyal. I graduated from Bianco to two other horses, the last of which was a grey called Gino and needed stabling. Farmer Freddie Whittingham owned fields up the Cymau, and we paid him for use of his field and stable.

Dad was a dab hand with horses and was happy to get up early with me. In the later days, with bigger, more expensive horses that needed better care, he would run me up the mountain to the stables first thing. I'd take the horses out into the field, organise the hay and food, walk back home, jump in the shower and then head to school. Once I got back home, I would collect Joanne and we'd go straight to the field, muck out the horses and take them to the stables. In winter, we'd make up horse feed of oats and barley, pouring boiling water on it and carrying it up to the field. Cleaning all the tack and polishing the riding equipment would take hours, but we relished it. Dad would meet us when he finished work. He wouldn't let me go hacking on my own, so I have lots of memories of trotting off into the horizon and looking over my shoulder to see Dad walking behind in the distance. Some weekends we'd cover many miles, but he'd always be there, keeping an eye on me.

I let Gino go when I turned seventeen and cars suddenly started to get faster. 'Horsepower' became something different and a whole lot scarier. We stayed in touch with Mr Whittingham, though, who, throughout my childhood, would give Joanne and me an orphaned lamb each in the spring. 'That one's yours,' he'd say, 'and that one's yours. You're in charge of feeding them and looking after them.' He would pass over milk bottles with big teats on the end, and we tended the lambs all the way through the season. Maybe he was just making light work for himself, but it made no difference to us.

Walking down the Cymau hill was where I saw a ghost. At dusk, Joanne and I were walking home from the stables and came to the sweeping bend. In front of us, at the bottom of the hill on the same side, was a man in full military uniform. He stopped, turned and looked up at us. He walked across the road and through the tall hedge, disappearing. I ran home panicked, shaking and refusing to sleep in my own bed.

'Don't be so silly,' Mum said.

She brought this up with Freddie Whittingham the next day.

'She's seen a ghost,' he said.

'What do you mean?'

'Where she's seen him – in full uniform – that used to be an air base. Kerry couldn't have known that.'

Nan and I researched it, and he was right. The air base wasn't even there in Freddie's lifetime.

My fame on the telly didn't start with my job at Wrexham. Aged fifteen, I got the opportunity to be an extra in *Brookside*, the Channel 4 soap opera set in Liverpool. My mum was friends with a chaperone to the children on the show, who got in touch to see if I'd like to be an extra, along with my cousin Mark. The scene was an acid house party hosted by Barry Grant, played by Paul Usher. We had to dance without music and then Usher's character pushed me out of the way as he was fleeing. It was a very strange experience, but I loved every minute of it. We were paid with a can of Coke and a Mars bar!

Otherwise, I never felt different to anybody throughout my childhood. My friends on the cul-de-sac didn't treat me differently and I didn't stand out at my first primary school, Ysgol Estyn Hope. When I was younger, the only time I was conscious of my disability was on my visits to see the specialist. After we moved, I built a life around Joanne and my pony, and even though I didn't have other friends at my new school, my childhood was filled with happy memories.

# CHAPTER TWO

# BULLIED

From the top of the stairs, I closed my eyes and screamed down to my parents: 'If you make me go to school tomorrow, I will kill myself. I'll do it. Don't make me go.'

This is how Sunday nights went. Everyone can recall from their own childhood those signals – a particular TV theme tune, the call to get in the bath, the street lights coming on – that heralded the end of the weekend and sent their heart sinking with the realisation that it was school tomorrow. My Sunday nights began with tantrums, breakdowns and anxiety. I would lock myself in the bathroom on Monday morning and try to make myself sick – but I never knew how to do it.

That is what bullying did to me.

I felt trapped in the house, too scared to go off the end of my drive where the bullies would sometimes congregate. I would look out of the window, see them there and be overcome with fear. I was terrified to even go the few doors down to Joanne's house.

Ian would confront them for me: 'Stop hanging around! Why are you here?' Relying on your younger brother to stand up for you adds another layer of humiliation.

I cannot thank God enough that when I was in school, no one had mobile phones or social media. If they had, I wouldn't be here now. I'm breaking down just writing that, but I can say with conviction that I wouldn't have survived. Yes, kids would be at the bottom of our drive, but I could still go home at night and shut the door. What would I have done if their words were in the house – in my bedroom, in the phone in my hand, at all hours of the day and night?

For my first two years of school, I thrived. Had I stayed at Ysgol Estyn, maybe things would have been different. As it was, we moved, when I was six, three miles up the road and we fell into a different catchment area. My new school was the catalyst for all my problems. Suddenly, I didn't fit in among children who had already formed tight friendship groups. I was an outsider, and so on the fringes that I would go home for dinner. My lifeline was Joanne, my only friend in the world. But, being a year younger, she would not be coming to secondary school with me. And that was where things really spiralled.

If pressed, I might have admitted that I did start Castell Alun High School with a great hope of meeting new people. But mostly, I felt anxiety. Without Joanne, I didn't find it easy to mix. I only knew the kids who had caused problems for me at primary school. Very quickly, others sensed my vulnerability. Kids often see differences as weakness. With my disability and bright red hair, they saw me as an easy target. And that view ripped through the year like a contagion.

My bullies would turn the other kids against me, and each day they would push and push and push – constantly, relentlessly, from 8.50 a.m. until 3.15 p.m. – until I broke down in tears. Even then, they never showed remorse. That I was weak enough to cry made it funnier for them. Some days, I would sob long into the evening and wake up for school the next day with my face puffy from crying.

My limp meant that I had a pass to use the lift between lessons, which only exacerbated things. When we'd line up outside class-rooms, I'd be the last in the line. Nobody would speak to me, and if they did, it would be to mimic me, dragging their legs behind them or walking on their tiptoes.

When I unconsciously pressed my thumb into the palm of my hand, as I had done since I was a baby, I felt so embarrassed that my arm didn't work properly that I would hide it in my coat pocket. I kept my coat on even at the height of summer. I'm sure I looked silly, but I had to know where my hand was. When it was in my pocket, no one could see it spasm. In my head, it was like a beacon flashing, drawing unwanted attention from bullies.

PE was the biggest struggle for me because I couldn't keep up with my classmates. My leg was painful. I was always last in the races and last to be picked for any team. I became a master of ex-cuses: I was waiting for a hospital appointment, I'd (deliberately) forgotten my PE kit or I wasn't well.

Kids never used my name at school. They called me Olive, from the ITV sitcom *On the Buses*: bright red hair, bob, thick prescription glasses and the target of everybody's abuse and jokes. Maybe that would have been funny the first time, but I was never in on the joke. When teachers called on me to answer questions, invariably some-one would interrupt: 'She's not Kerry! She's Olive!' Everyone would laugh. No teacher ever challenged them. It was like they hadn't heard the same words I had. And in the end, teachers stopped asking me to contribute in class because they didn't want to deal with the dis-ruption that followed. That kind of erasure – to not even be granted the dignity of your own name – is a deceptively powerful thing. It left me invisible, in more ways than one.

School days passed with me keeping silent. I didn't dare put my hand up to answer anything. I dreaded the rare moments when teachers asked me anything directly because I would give an answer and people would laugh and sneer.

I could do nothing right. Everything I did drew criticism, comments and name-calling. I would sit on my own, and if anyone did deign to reach out to me, they'd be rebuked: 'What are you talking to her for?' The silence – the isolation – was almost as hard as all the attention. I would wake up each morning and simply not know how I was going to get through the day.

My cerebral palsy has affected parts of my brain, including my memory. We didn't know that at the time, but it explains why I didn't find schoolwork easy. On a scan, parts of my brain show up black where they have been damaged. There was no such thing as learning support in my mainstream school back then. Teachers often said that I would have scored top marks if I'd been able to talk my way through exams, but my written work was disorganised and chaotic because I struggled to translate my thoughts to paper.

It didn't help that I was simply too terrified to focus. I was so exhausted emotionally with getting through the day that there was nothing left in me to devote to schoolwork. How could I be interested in learning when I hated every minute of life in that place? I was too scared to go to the toilet, so frightened of who might be waiting for me that I would hold it in all day. At home time, I would run up the road, hammer on the front door and dance on the top step until Mum opened the door – that's how much of my life I put on hold.

In my role now, I work with children who attend a fabulous special needs school in Wrexham, St Christopher's. I look back and wish it had existed when I was a kid, because these children are so happy, understood and supported. At my school, I would be in tears by 9 a.m. I was a regular visitor to the school nurse with stomach cramps and mystery illnesses. Sometimes I wasn't faking anything because the stress and anxiety of it all would make me feel terrible. She would ring home right away and call my mum: 'Can you come and pick Kerry up?'

I never stood up to my bullies. I never argued back. I didn't have that in me. I look back and think that I didn't try hard enough to fit in. I often think I let myself be the victim. But I'm looking back with adult eyes – as the strong Kerry who would never allow herself to be pushed around and would let their words wash over me. I have to remind myself that it's not so easy when you're a child. What do you do if you're not invited to sit with somebody? No one asked me to their table. Kids would get up and move if I joined them.

I was endlessly analysing what I'd done wrong. I must have done something – why, otherwise, would they pick me? It had to be my fault. Maybe that's why I just accepted the torment as inevitable. And the longer it went on, the lower I felt. How do you come back from lows like that? Just surviving was hard enough.

I felt like I was in the wrong and that I had to grow a backbone if I had any hope of making any of it stop. Nobody talked about mental health then, but of course I was suffering. As a teenager I felt like no one was helping me, that no one was on my side. I used to wonder if it would be easier if the bullying were physical: then, people would have seen bruises. As it was, it felt impossible to get anyone to understand how deep my pain ran.

Mum has said in the years since that she is sorry that she didn't find a new school for me. I only learned years later that she went to have meetings with the school. 'If Kerry's a child that's bullied, she'll always be a child that's bullied,' said the school doctor. 'Moving schools won't help. The bullying will just move with her.'

I never bought that. A new place with new people would have been a fresh start. But that was the school's logic, and as a result, it was my mum's. All my parents really had was the approach typical of the time: to tell me I had to go to school. Mum would tell me that if I didn't go, she'd be in trouble. As kids, we knew about the man in a white van, the 'wag man' (otherwise known as the truancy officer), who would come knocking.

'You've got to stand up for yourself,' she'd say. 'We can't fight your battles for you, unfortunately.' My parents did everything possible to support me through those times, but they were helpless themselves. In my first year of secondary school, there was no option of a bus there, so my mum learned to drive specifically so that I didn't have to walk the distance with my bad leg. When the bullying was at its worst, her driving served a different purpose. She would drop me off at 8.45 a.m., collect me for dinner, then pick me up again at 3.15 p.m. She couldn't have done more, yet I still was, in my hours at school, isolated and lonely.

Mum also had a meeting with the school nurse.

'This happens with people who've got a disability that's not pronounced,' the nurse said. 'Kids who wear glasses, have big teeth, walk with a limp – they're fair game. If your daughter was in a wheelchair, they'd look after her.'

Now that I'm older, I completely understand how difficult this time was for my parents, too. They felt guilty and helpless themselves because they couldn't save me from being bullied. But my parents had to send me to school no matter how much I screamed that I didn't want to go. They would sit with me at night as I sobbed myself to sleep.

This was all new to Mum and Dad. Their second child was Ian: super popular, he achieved top marks in everything he did and had people queuing around the block to ask him to come and play. He was the ringmaster of his friendship groups, the first picked for football matches and the star of Mum's dancing school. Ian was such a big character that no one would dare pick on him for dancing: the neighbourhood just accepted that he would play football on a Sunday morning and go to ballet in the afternoon. I was jealous of his easy confidence and the respect he commanded. Why did I have to go through all that pain and he didn't? I struggled to find my own sense of self while he seemed to know himself so effortlessly.

My youngest brother, Matt, was born while I was at secondary school. I was excited about welcoming a new baby to the family, but, of course, no one at school would let me be. 'Ew – that's disgusting!' they'd say. 'Your mum and dad are having a baby? You're thirteen!'

My science teacher's wife was also pregnant. I would sit there silently begging him not to mention the baby, but he always did: 'How is your Mum, Kerry? How much longer until the baby's due?' My heart would sink; I knew what would follow. My bullies turned something so wonderful and special into something sordid and horrible.

Matt's arrival was a lonely time for me because Mum was poorly after giving birth and was in hospital for weeks after Matt came home. Nan and Granddad would be at our house every night when we arrived home from school, sorting out the tea and looking after us until Dad would arrive home from work. When he left again in the morning, our grandparents would return early to get us ready for school and then take over looking after a newborn all day. I could hardly go to them with my problems at that time.

My only ally was Mrs Hartlepayne, the cookery teacher and the one person who sensed how hard I was finding school. She knew I didn't have any friends and would invite me to have my dinner with her in her classroom. She would be subtle and sensitive: 'The class just gone have rushed out and left a sink full of dishes, Kerry. Can you wash them for me?' Gladly! I relished the safety of her classroom – the safety of her.

Joanne joined the school in my second year, but her presence didn't bring the reprieve I'd been longing for. We always went together on the bus, but she was in a different year and had her own circle of friends to spend break and dinnertime with. She would always be there when I needed her and happily let me tag along with her group, but that still didn't bring me a feeling of belonging because they were *her* friends. Joanne aside, I didn't have anyone who valued me for who I was. To my self-conscious teenage mind, it felt very obvious that I was following her with no idea of how to keep up.

After school, however, we were inseparable. We'd get home at 3.25 p.m. and twenty minutes later, Joanne and I would be together.

On Friday night and Saturday, I could enjoy life. At thirteen, I was paid £14 a week at my Saturday job at a petrol station from noon to 7 p.m., but I didn't want to work on my own. I would split the money with Joanne and we'd chat all through the shift. I wouldn't have done it without her. There was pony club on Sunday morning, and we'd spend any spare hours at each other's houses.

The minute her front door closed, though, the terror would start. I'd look at the twelve doors between her house and mine and scan the street for any of my tormentors from school. Then I'd run. I would count the door numbers, panting and checking over my shoulder, waiting for relief. Finally, I'd skid onto our drive and slam the front door. I was safe.

The bullies did become a source of tension in my relationship with Joanne. I never confronted her about it, but I was always disappointed that she never stood up for me. Worse, while I wanted to run as far away as possible if I saw my bullies in the street, Joanne would stop and say hello to them. That felt like the most enormous betrayal. Why did she do it? Why did she even acknowledge them? Why didn't she help me? But they'd never done anything to her. Now, with adult eyes, I can see it differently: it wasn't her battle to fight. Being friends with me didn't make her enemies with them. We'll be mates forever, but back then, she was all I had.

Where Joanne had a thriving social life, I opted out of everything. I wouldn't go to school discos, shows or residentials. That's what bullying does to you. I spent what could have been some of the best years of my life just trying to avoid trouble, knowing that no one would miss me anyway. While other teenagers thumbed through college prospectuses and made calls about apprenticeships, my only hope was to get as far away as I could from the kids I'd been with. I even did my work experience at Dad's company because I was terrified of having to meet people who would be as cruel to me as my tormentors at school.

The final day of school was the happiest of my life. We had a leavers' assembly, which my mum came to, but I ducked out of the egg and flour fights and didn't ask anyone to sign my shirt. I couldn't get out of there fast enough. Getting over the threshold and through the school gate for the last time was my only focus.

It took longer for my mind to feel free. For years afterwards, I had a recurring nightmare that I was trapped in school. I dreamt of the school's big double gates and smaller side gates; it was always the last day and, in my haste to be free, I'd trip, flying from the campus and landing outside. I'd wake with a start, my heart racing.

I wonder what my bullies would think, as adults, about what happened all those years ago. Would they be sorry? Would they be embarrassed? Would they not remember everything in the way I have? They must regret that time, the impact that they had on my childhood and the far-reaching consequences of all they said and did.

I still carry that pain with me. I still feel the anger and the sadness, and I wonder if I will ever get over it. Recently, I was invited to a party for my friend Will's fiftieth; I turned down the invitation initially because I couldn't face going back to those days. In the end, Will sent over his guest list so that I could check who would be there. At fifty, I'm still terrified of reliving what I went through as a kid. For anti-bullying week one year, I ran a full week of campaigns at Wrexham. Looking ahead, I would love to go into schools, with the backing of the football club, to explain to children how damaging their words can be.

Casey, my daughter, blossomed at school: she was popular, picked for the lead roles in the school plays, had perfect grades. She was just like her uncle Ian was at her age. The minute she fell out with other kids, though, I would start researching new schools. Twice I went and looked around them. I wasn't going to leave her to endure what I had.

That was my reflex reaction, but it wasn't what Casey needed, and it wasn't fair to laden her school years with all of the trauma I still carried from mine. It might sound strange, but I'm very jealous of Casey because she got to have the experiences that I never did. I missed out on all the things at school that made her the person she is. And I didn't know that I was missing out when I was living it – I was just waiting for it all to end.

Back then, at fifteen, I didn't know that my time at school would bring a life sentence of anxiety and low self-esteem. I simply took it for granted that I was worthless, that I was a nobody and that was all I would ever be. A core belief had formed. In just a few years' time, it would wreak further havoc on me.

# CHAPTER THREE

# BREAKING FREE

*Please be aware that this chapter contains depictions of domestic violence and rape, which some readers may find distressing.*

I turned sixteen on 5 August 1991. I'd enjoyed my weeks of freedom after leaving school, but it was soon time to start thinking about what I would be doing next.

Most of the kids I'd been to school with were enrolling at Yale College, now Coleg Cambria, but I was adamant that I wasn't going. You couldn't have paid me to go anywhere with the people who had given me so much trouble. I was half-heartedly looking at admin courses at colleges further afield, but in truth, I didn't really know what I wanted to do. Still, I wasn't fretting about the future because I was simply overcome with the relief of leaving behind the chapter that had brought me so much pain. I certainly hadn't left school with big ambitions for my life, although I was keen to go to the workplace and start earning.

'You've got to go out there and find a full-time job for yourself,' went my mum's refrain in the weeks after I left school. 'No one is going to knock on the door and offer you one.' The irony is, that's exactly what happened.

My Auntie Alice had six sons who together had built up a car dealership with sites in Wrexham and Queensferry into a franchise called Lindop Brothers. My mum's cousin, David, was the CEO of the branch in Bradley, Wrexham.

He materialised at the end of the garden path one day: 'Hiya, Sue. Has your Kerry finished school this year? Is she looking for a job? We're looking for a receptionist.'

That was the start of my working life. I was extraordinarily lucky, because my lack of confidence meant that I wouldn't have been the best at interviews. But I knew how to answer David's questions: I have, I am and thank you very much – when can I start?

I was nervous at the thought of stepping into a new, male-dominated world. I would be one of only three women at the company, and would be sat near the service manager, Nige, at the end of a sweeping desk. I would take home £65 a week for answering the phones, sorting the mail and directing people to the correct department.

I found work liberating and refreshing because none of my colleagues knew what I had been through. It was like I'd pressed delete on any backstory and history. I don't know if I would have found that freedom at college, around people my own age, but at the car dealership, I didn't have any reputation – as 'girl, bullied' – following me. My coworkers, all years older than me, felt so removed from my previous life and all the trauma that had come with it. The cleaner was in her fifties, as was the lady in admin. The salesmen were in their twenties and thirties and were going home to their own partners and families. I didn't have to consciously reinvent myself. Instead, I found instant acceptance for who I was.

At 3.30 p.m. every afternoon, Joanne would call my desk and tell me that she had just got home from school. Those moments reminded me that I was in a bigger world, away from algebra and textbooks and hiding at dinnertime, and on the first step of the ladder to independence. The work was simple, but I found it fulfilling and took it seriously. If 1,500 letters needed posting, I would take home the ones I hadn't got round to during the day and sit stuffing envelopes at the dining room table. That drive was a side to me that had never come out at school, where I'd put in the bare minimum effort to scrape by. When I was engaged with something, I was like a dog with a bone. I could contribute. I had something to offer.

Work brought with it a social life as I made friends with the staff from the service and sales teams. At the end of a handful of nights out, whoever had the keys for the dealership – certainly not me – would open up the garage and we'd hang around there until the small hours with pizzas. We never did any harm, but sorry, Dave, if you're now reading this! I had a short relationship with my first boyfriend, who was working in the factory down the road. That fizzled out after a little while, but I felt like I was finding my feet in life – like new worlds were opening up for me.

When I was seventeen, Sian, just a couple of years older than me, came to work in the parts department. As the two youngest members of the team, we gravitated towards each other. I admired this confident, independent woman who could drive and, most impressively, had her own flat, in Ruabon. 'Come to my house for the weekend,' she winked one day.

Being seventeen and still living with my parents, this was intoxicating. Suddenly, for two whole days, I didn't have to be back for tea or tucked in bed when Mum and Dad said so. In fact, I wasn't answerable to anybody. Was this grown-up life? All this freedom and all this choice?

Sian had a second job in the local off-licence some evenings, and I arrived at her flat one weekend to find that she'd called one of her old schoolfriends to come and babysit me. 'I'm Kings,' he said.

We spent that night, without Sian, just chatting away. We hit it off instantly. Kings was easy-going, funny and definitely very likeable.

Our friendship developed a life of its own away from Sian, and after only a short time, we were doing everything together. I would call Kings and ask him to pick me up and he would take me to his mum's house to stay the night, me in his bed and him on the sofa. Kings's mum, Barbara, was one of those people so laid-back as to be horizontal, and she would welcome me with the words: 'Here she is again! You can have his bed!'

In the early days, they would laugh at me for living in what they called a 'posh house'; Kings's family had a council house without central heating. Barbara would wet herself laughing as I rocked up in a pair of pyjamas and all my extra layers: I'd get into my sleeping bag, wrap my throw blanket around it and then burrow under Kings's duvet. 'Well,' she'd say, watching me roll myself up in my cocoon. 'Nothing's ever going to happen with you two, is it?'

I would sit and have Sunday dinner still wearing my coat, watching ice form on the inside of the single glazed windows, spreading so far as to reduce the view to small circles. Kings would walk around in his T-shirt, shaking his head at me.

A real highlight with the Evans family was Pancake Day, when the whole family would pile into Barbara's and she'd make pancakes for hours. 'It's your tea!' she'd say. Everyone looked forward to this yearly tradition, including Casey, when she was younger. Pancake Day has never been the same since Barbara's passing.

Kings spent Christmas with me and my family twice. Instead of one present, there would be twelve, and each was a bracelet or a necklace. By that point, he was a fixture in our family. He'd bunk down in Matt's bedroom, and he knew everything and everyone.

Kings says now that, from the moment he met me, he knew that he wanted us to be together. He would ask me to be his girlfriend, and each time I would turn him down. 'No, no,' I'd say. 'We're not going to get together because we're friends. If we become a couple and it ends, we'll lose our friendship. I'm just not willing to risk that. You're too important to me. You're too much to lose.'

Mum and Joanne would watch all this unfold with disbelief. 'Don't be so silly, Kerry!' Mum would say. 'He's absolutely gorgeous. And he worships you. Why don't you just say yes?' Even Joanne, who was always so laid-back and usually happy to let me get on with things, couldn't resist trying to twist my arm. 'You and Kings are made for each other,' she'd insist. 'He's so lovely. You're not going to get better than him.'

Then I got into my second relationship. But not with Kings.

I'd known Shane – not his real name – from life in the village. I would see him in the garage where I'd worked as a teenager. He was related to a friend I'd known for a long time.

My relationship with Shane was the first time I was infatuated. He was absolutely wonderful. I was obsessed with him and was constantly daydreaming about him, waiting for him to call and planning what to say when we'd next be together. Life became about winding down the hours until I'd see him.

Mum and Dad didn't see what I did.

I had just spent several years being made to feel worthless. All I wanted was love. Love, and acceptance, and everything I'd never got at school. I had never been liked, and I wanted to be wanted. And here was a beautiful boy who loved me – who loved me so badly that he wanted me to move in with him. It was a jolt, given I had never felt good enough for Shane. How could I, after all I had been through? How had I got so lucky? How had I found someone who wanted to be with me?

We found a house to rent, and I felt like I was floating as I went around my parents' house packing my things on moving day. As Shane and I shifted boxes and tossed each other the parcel tape, Mum sat in the lounge and didn't come out. I was indifferent to her advice: don't do it, because it will all end in tears. That day, I never once considered my parents' feelings. I was earning my own money, and I told them that I could do what I liked. I was headstrong; I knew exactly what – and who – I wanted and where I needed to be.

Then he hit me for the first time.

We were spending the evening with Joanne and her boyfriend. They had gone upstairs and Shane and I planned to stay overnight downstairs. Neither of us was drunk. When he turned around and smacked my face, it came completely out of the blue. It just happened from nothing.

I felt the blood run down my face as, shaking, I turned back to him.

'I can't believe you've done this,' I breathed. Instantly, he changed, turning back into the Shane I knew and loved. The anger vanished as quickly as it arrived. 'I'm so, so sorry,' he sobbed, reaching for me. 'I won't do that again, I promise.'

Joanne woke up the next morning to find my blood downstairs. Shane and I had disappeared into the night in the back of a taxi.

It was always the last time – until the next one. Then the apologies would start again. He was always sorry. He would never do it again. On he went, reading from the same script that women have heard for generations and generations, reciting all the clichés right on cue: *I love you. I can't be without you. Please don't leave me.* I would watch him cry – this man that I was besotted with – and I wanted so desperately to believe him. I wanted so badly for his words to be true that I lied to myself in order to make them so. I look back now and want to shout through the years: *Run, Kerry. He's shown you who he is.*

Things could be normal for weeks at a time until he would explode over the tiniest things – and always, always when he'd had a drink. The first sign that anything was brewing would be the impact of his fist on my face. He hit me and I bled. He hit me and gave me bruises. Then he hit me again. The week he gave me two black eyes, I called Mum and Dad and made up a long-winded excuse about why I couldn't come to see them.

'You need to get out, Kerry,' Kings would say. 'That's nothing to do with us being in a relationship – that's for your own wellbeing. It's not safe. I don't know anyone who treats women like that.'

I shook my head. I wanted my relationship to work more than anything. I didn't want everyone to be right. I was still seeing the best in Shane. I was in denial: I wanted things to just be normal and thought that I would be able to fix him. Yes, working life had changed me, but underneath, I was still so profoundly damaged, so desperate to be loved that I was blinded to Shane's true character.

'I'm not a fighter, but I'll go around there and have him,' Kings would say. I would beg him not to. In the end, we came to a compromise. 'Look,' Kings said. 'If you need to get out of there for any reason, just ring. It doesn't matter to me. I'll come out. If I can, I will help you. I'll pick you up for an hour – just to get you out of that place.'

• • •

I had turned out the bedroom lights when I felt Shane moving next to me. He pinned my wrists to either side of my head.

'No,' I said. I remember so clearly saying this. 'No. No. I don't want to.'

I believe so strongly that sexual abuse – rape – is the worst, most terrifying thing anybody could ever go through. It is the total loss of control – to be so overpowered that you are helpless, completely at the mercy of someone else. No matter how many times I protested, Shane continued. He was absolutely, utterly beyond reason.

'Get off me! Get off me!'

In the dark, I lay shaking as Shane sprawled next to me in silence. I listened to his breathing: he was sleeping. He thought so little of me that after what he had done, he could just go to sleep. The words came to me with a clarity and conviction: *I can't do this anymore. I can't. I'm worth more. I've got to get away. He is not going to change. I've got to do something about this, or I will be his victim for the rest of my life.*

I watched the rise and fall of Shane's chest. When I was sure he was in a deep enough sleep, I crept down the hallway and looked at the clock. 12.30 a.m. I dialled Kings. 'I need to get out of here,' I whispered. 'Now. I can't stay.'

I remember the fear, knowing that I couldn't be in the flat a moment longer in case Shane woke up. I didn't take anything but my coat. In the small hours, I sat on the wall outside in the dark and waited for Kings. Shane had hit me until I'd bled, given me bruises beneath both of my eyes, but this would be the final time. What had happened was so traumatic, so horrendous, that there was simply no going back.

A few days later, Kings came to the flat with me to collect my few belongings. I existed in a haze. These things always happen to somebody else, don't they? No, because this time it had happened to me. I was in genuine disbelief, battling against the dawning horror of knowing that my life had changed.

Like many abuse survivors, I blamed myself. I should have listened to what my friends and family were telling me, and I should have known better. There are things that happen to you and things you choose to do, and I had made the decision to put myself in that situation. I had got myself into that mess. And I'd done that because of what had happened to me at school. So many people had knocked me. So many people had told me that I was worthless. That's why I'd rushed into a relationship where nothing was as it seemed. I had just wanted somebody to love me.

I never reported what had happened to me. I didn't think that I would win, not against someone so charismatic. I already knew how good he was at twisting things and making me think that I was the one in the wrong. Which one of us would be believed?

It is the only regret I have in life. I could have done something, and I didn't because I was too scared. I wish I had got that closure for myself. I have heard since, via that whisper network that women form to protect each other from the men we should never be alone with, that Shane has made other victims, and I wonder if I could have stopped him if I'd said something. But I was a different person then. It's easy to think all this on the other side, when someone else has built me back up.

I wish I could tell younger Kerry, in those first shell-shocked days, that I would find myself and emerge stronger from it all. I would get back my self-esteem, learn to see that the world isn't all so terrifying and discover that it doesn't matter what other people think and that joy won't always crumble like sand. Someone was on hand to teach me that – the one who had been there all along.

# CHAPTER FOUR

# KINGS AND CASEY

*Please be aware that this chapter contains descriptions of baby loss, which some readers may find distressing.*

The woman who emerged from that relationship with Shane was shattered.

'Nobody is ever going to want me,' I said to Kings on one particularly low day.

'Well, I do,' Kings replied. He knew that I knew this, and he knew, too, not to push it. I just couldn't see myself kissing Kings. Moreover, the thought of losing a best friend, after all I'd lost already, should things fall apart once we took it further, was too much to bear.

Kings knew that to keep asking would put his feelings in the way of what we had. I just assumed that he would go off, find somebody else and none of my feelings would change. But he kept hoping. Everyone around us could see what I couldn't and told me as much: my perfect match was right in front of my eyes. 'You are being silly, Kerry,' Mum said as we took the plates into the kitchen after one Sunday dinner. 'He's your rock. He's right under your nose. He's so desperate to be with you.'

Things changed when we shared a slow, nervous kiss one night in front of the TV. Kings went home and I called Joanne to help me process my emotions. Most people might have felt that development was a natural progression of such a close and treasured friendship, but I just couldn't see that. It felt like the kiss had come out the blue – a momentary aberration. One that, if I could bring myself to admit it, I'd enjoyed.

'He's going to be amazing,' Joanne gushed. 'You need to be with him. He's absolutely perfect for you.'

The only crack in those early days together was that Shane's actions still cast a shadow. If Kings and I were playfighting and he pinned me down, I'd panic, screaming and forcing him off me. Kings had borne witness to my trauma and knew that we had to take things slowly, and he handled me delicately as the relationship moved at my pace. Kings was at ease with himself and the world and wasn't bothered by what people thought about him. He taught me to look at life in the same way. Over time, this woman who had always been riddled with anxiety and agonised over whether people were looking at her was filled with new confidence as she learned anew how to enjoy living. That was all down to Kings.

Never had someone treated me as well as Kings did. He had always been a steady hand, and I'd never wanted that. More accurately, I'd never *realised* I'd wanted that. Even as a friend, he showered me with compliments and gifts – big things like necklaces and small things like bars of chocolate – to make it known that he was thinking of me and that I meant the world to him. After Shane, that was the most welcome, surprising change.

At first, I resisted Kings's compliments because I've always struggled with my self-esteem, but Kings made me feel worthy. Most of all, I loved his company. Our days together were peaceful and content.

• • •

I'd suffered from terrible stomach problems since my teens, and I'd unsuccessfully fought for years for a diagnosis of Crohn's disease. I was always in pain, struggling with bloating, constipation and diarrhoea, and constantly in and out of hospital. It had got particularly bad in the summer of 1997. That was the reason why, on a family holiday to Blackpool with Joanne in September, I laid on the floor and ordered her to stand on my stomach so that I could fit into an unexpectedly tight pair of jeans. We went out clubbing and drank all night, but the bloating persisted for weeks. After more visits to the doctor's surgery, a GP listened to my symptoms, felt my stomach and finally prescribed me medication for Crohn's.

It was only in November that we realised – I was seven and a half months pregnant. Our baby was due in February.

As we scrambled to ready the house for parenthood, the midwife visited on Christmas Eve for her final rounds before the holidays. She listened to my stomach and asked me questions, and I thought I'd passed the test with flying colours. The midwife's hand was on the door handle when Mum said: 'Have you told her that you've been spotting?'

What happened next lives in my memory as a series of hazy snapshots. Hospital, immediately. Delivery suite. Someone used the words 'emergency caesarean'. The placenta had pulled away and was starving the baby. Then I was bleeding heavily, the sheets turning red beneath me. All I knew, in those moments, was urgency and my love for a child about to be born so prematurely that none of us knew whether they would survive. I didn't process, then, whether I would be present to experience my own giving birth. My only focus was our unborn baby's life.

General anaesthetic. Theatre. Blackness.

I woke up, alone, to a Polaroid picture on the bedside table: a daughter, who I would not be able to see until Christmas Day, in the afternoon. Our Casey.

'We didn't even know if she'd survive the night,' Kings said when he came to see me in those first confusing hours. He explained that Casey had stopped breathing half a dozen times and they'd had to restart her heart. She would need a course of injections to mature her lungs.

While I had been under, Kings and Mum had endured the un-imaginable stress of waiting on the fate of two people they loved – one of whom they'd never met. Kings was grateful that Mum took charge: Mum is a list person, an organiser, and held them both together while his mind surged between pure elation to absolute terror. Now, on the mother and baby ward – where I was the only mother without her baby – he had settled on a cautious, wary joy. As newborns wailed behind us, my presence there felt incongruous. But it would be a whole day before I would see Casey myself.

On Christmas afternoon, Joanne visited. Kings had gone to his mum's and my mum was hosting Nan and Granddad. In the strangely silent hospital, the nurses allowed Joanne to see me out-side of visiting hours, and she pushed me in a wheelchair down to the unit for premature babies.

And that was the first time I saw Casey.

'This can't be my baby,' I said. 'Mine will have red hair.' Once I'd gotten over my surprise at the smattering of dark hair on her head, I slid open the side of the incubator, rested my fingers by her hand and stroked her with one finger. Like all mothers, that was the moment when life made sense. Instantly, Casey became my world.

Nan had knitted three different hats for the day Casey left hospital, but they were all too big. The new hat Casey wore in her incubator was made to fit a satsuma. Born at just over 3 lbs, Casey, as many babies do, dropped weight – but she was so little, she didn't have any weight to lose. When I would put my hand under her to wind her, she was so light and fragile that it was as though a little bird was on my shoulder.

On the prem unit, my every action was scrutinised. I was just twenty-two with my first baby, whereas other mothers were welcoming their second or third, and I felt very immature by comparison. A nurse supervised me the first time I held Casey and the first time I fed her – with a tube because she couldn't be bottle fed. When I was discharged, I stayed with Mum and Dad, and Dad used to run me to the hospital each morning so that I could sit with Casey while he and Kings went off to work. When Casey was finally well enough to leave, nurses had to assess me to see that I knew how to look after her. I did – and our wonderful new life could begin.

● ● ●

'Don't even ask to marry me,' Kings insisted for years. He was a child of divorce, and, in his eyes, marriages always ended in break-ups. Kings didn't want the hassle of marriage when we were as good as husband and wife anyway. It took a long time for him to feel ready, but then one day it all made sense for him.

For months, I'd been telling Kings that I needed a new wardrobe.

One afternoon, he crouched down on one knee at the side of the settee. 'Do you want to go shopping tomorrow for a new wardrobe? I've got the money – or you can have an engagement ring.'

It was hardly whistling me away to Paris with roses! I should have known what I was getting into by choosing somebody as down-to-earth as Kings.

'Really? You're offering me a wardrobe or a ring?'

'Seriously,' he said. 'I want to marry you.'

Even Kings's mum was sceptical when I returned to her house that Friday night and told her the news. 'Yeah, right,' she said. 'Wait until he's sober in the morning.' By the third day, I knew that he meant it for real. I chose the ring.

Mum and I went into overdrive and planned the wedding of my dreams in under six months. I had the most perfect, special day with a hotel wedding at Rossett Hall, generously paid for by my parents.

I told Kings that there were three things he had to do. One: be at the right place. Two: arrive on time. Three: pick our first dance. As time went on, I agonised over this last one. What if he chose some horrendous club tune? Again, I should have trusted him from the start – we danced to Madonna's 'Crazy For You'.

Joanne, being my best friend, was my maid of honour along with Lowri, Kings's niece. Dad was used to public speaking through his job and gave the most touching, perfect speech, joking that my Little Ted would have to move aside to make room for my husband. Kings's best man, Phil, said he could never follow such a brilliant speech, toasted the bride and groom and promptly sat back down.

Four-year-old Casey was also a bridesmaid and had spent weeks looking forward to a night of dancing. When the big night came, she toddled over to us after half an hour and tugged at my dress: 'Can I go to bed now?'

Mum had volunteered to take her up to bed, but the only person she wanted was her daddy. Kings had to leave his own wedding party to put her to bed, and Mum then took over as Kings returned to his wedding celebrations.

'The best way to be with somebody is as a friend first,' I'd always tell Casey as she got older. 'You've got so much history.'

As a young girl, you expect the fairy-tale wedding: the big castle and the white horse. The reality is that romance can be found in far more mundane things. On the eve of our wedding, Kings enjoyed a rowdy last night of freedom at home. When we woke up and entered the front room, it was like a bomb had gone off. Kings said that he'd spent the small hours of the morning panicking. 'I'm getting married and I need to clean up!' he'd shouted to his stags. The romance of our day fizzled out very quickly, but Kings knew that we'd have a lifetime together to tidy.

We had a honeymoon together in Tenerife, which was the first time we'd ever left Casey behind to go on holiday. My mum and Barbara had her that week and spoiled her.

The only thing missing in our lives was a sibling for Casey.

I had miscarried before our wedding at twelve weeks. Then I was pregnant with twins. Life was falling into place. Kings and I had picked out a newly renovated home, and, as we climbed the six stone steps to the front door, I explained to Casey how her mum would be having two babies. 'How will we manage up all these steps with a double pram?' I asked Kings afterwards.

I lost the twins at eighteen weeks. I lost a fourth baby at twenty weeks.

We were desperate to have more children. Each birthday and Christmas Casey would write her list and the request was the same: a brother or sister. And we couldn't give her one. It was blow after blow after blow.

Then there was Lewis. As his due date edged closer, hope began to build. Twenty-seven weeks. Twenty-eight weeks.

Then Lewis stopped kicking. And the bleeding started.

In hospital, I was told that Lewis had died. I would have to come back in the next day to give birth to him. I went home that night knowing that the baby inside me wasn't breathing.

It was crushing – absolutely crushing. I can't even describe the pain. It was probably the hardest thing that's ever happened to me. Our baby was nearly here. He was only a few weeks younger than Casey had been when she was born. We had so nearly made it. A few weeks was the difference between a healthy child and a dead one.

It was a kind of double grief: of grieving for all the love I had felt for Lewis and for the future we would never have. I was floored by the irony of it all. With all of these pregnancies I had done everything right; Casey had been the surprise, and I couldn't have done anything more wrong. It was a miracle that she survived.

For days, I didn't get dressed. There is no grief like miscarriage and stillbirth. When my grandparents were reaching their end, I talked to them and witnessed the moment they moved on. I've seen death. I've grieved. None of that compares to losing a baby.

It is a uniquely lonely time. People do not discuss your dead children with you because they don't know what to say. I felt very, very alone with my grief. No one allowed us to have a funeral and I felt cheated by that. We were denied the opportunity to grieve not only by silence and stigma but also by this refusal. No one pointed us in the direction of any kind of support. Kings and I were left to pull ourselves up by our bootstraps.

Kings's way of coping was to put the memory of it all in a box in his mind and never open it. I held Lewis after the birth, but Kings didn't feel able to be there. He couldn't bring himself to talk about it, not because he felt he had to man up but because to do so was so searingly, achingly painful. That, too, added to the loneliness I felt. Maybe it's different for a mother: I had felt Lewis inside me. I couldn't block out any of those feelings.

There's a spot up the Panorama near Llangollen with the most beautiful view that has always been special to Kings and me. In the absence of a funeral, we chose a tree there as our place to go and think about Lewis. A few years ago, Casey came to me on what would have been Lewis's birthday with a picture: she and her partner, Rhys, had left flowers at Lewis's tree.

Granddad died in March 2006, aged eighty-two, six months after my cerebral bleed. For the twelve months previous, he had complained of headaches, and he eventually entered hospital with an infection in his brain. The prognosis was hopeful, but over the next few weeks, Granddad deteriorated piece by piece. A once sprightly man was interacting with things nobody else could see. He would show signs of improvement only to be incoherent the next day. By the end, a tracheostomy had left him struggling to talk. When the doctors turned off the life support machine, I took comfort from knowing that he was no longer in pain. It broke my heart because we had had a very close relationship. He and Nan were my everything.

The family brought flowers for his coffin, and together his great-grandchildren picked out a teddy. After the cremation, Auntie Carol and Uncle Glyn came to me, united in the same thought: 'Don't leave the teddy here. Take it. For Lewis.' We left it in our special place to remember him.

Casey has always known about Lewis. We hadn't bought much before his birth because we were wary of what had happened before, but a friend gave me a cross-stitch of a bear sitting on a cloud embroidered with the words: 'Good night, sleep tight, Lewis'. We also have a Cherished Teddy figurine called Lewis, and printed on its base is a small poem: 'Though we might part, you'll always be in my heart'. It is one of the most treasured things I own.

With Lewis came the realisation that Kings and I would not have any more children. People miscarry and go on to have healthy babies, but what happened with Lewis felt final. Kings put it best: it's not that you ever stop wanting more children, but you give up the possible heartache that goes with trying and not having them. We didn't want the suffering and the pain any more.

I put the love I had to give into other avenues. When Casey was younger, I didn't want to leave her to work, so I took the relevant courses and became a childminder for vulnerable children. Those were some of the happiest times of our lives. 'We look after them, don't we, Mum?' Casey would say, as I explained, in appropriate terms, about some of the experiences these children had had.

In recent years, as the menopause approaches, I've probably devoted more headspace to thinking about my pregnancies. I was never going to have more children, but I still felt a kind of grief that the option had been taken from me: I couldn't have children even if I had wanted to. Maybe it's a biological thing, or maybe a little fragment of me had held onto hope all those years.

Everybody's child is their world, but I always felt like Casey means that little bit more to me because of everything that has happened since. In all honesty, she shouldn't be here. We are incredibly, in-credibly lucky.

I sometimes wonder if I've put more pressure on Casey because of all that. She has a successful career, was a popular and likeable child, was Mary in the nativity, always won events on sports days. I put her on a pedestal, and I wonder if she is fearful of failing and falling off it. In any case, I'm extraordinarily proud of her, and in awe of all she has achieved.

# CHAPTER FIVE

# THE CEREBRAL BLEED

## SEPTEMBER 2005

I am floating.

That is the sensation I have when I wake up in Wrexham Maelor Hospital. On the right side of my body, I feel nothing. It doesn't feel like my right arm and leg are there. I look down and see them, but bodily I have no awareness of them. I ask Kings to lightly pinch me in the hope of sparking some kind of sensation but it's like he's swiping at air. Hence the floating. It feels like I am lying suspended above the mattress.

I wait on a ward with patients with a range of conditions, each already assigned their own consultant. Most of them are elderly. One has already passed away during our time here. I haven't decorated my bed with cards or flowers, amplifying the feeling that this is all temporary. I am just waiting, waiting, waiting.

I replay again the last things I can remember, combing through the fragments of memory. A few scenes solidify. I remember collecting Casey from school. Coming home for the weekend. Walking to the kitchen to make tea. Opening the fridge for milk. The bottle falling through my hand. Collapsing to the floor. Then everything goes black.

Kings does his best to fill in the blanks. As I'd hit the floor, he flipped into crisis mode and called the ambulance while his mum came over to take Casey and shield her from whatever was about to unfold. I was talking as I came to, Kings says, but dazedly. My sentences were jumbled, my words in the wrong order.

That was one of the reasons why, Kings explains, the doctors think I could have had a stroke. But they're not sure. In any case, I can't bring myself to believe them. Don't strokes happen to old people? How can whatever happened to me be that serious?

Each day, a host of doctors sweep in and out of my room suggesting another round of tests or some different scans. I never hear about the results, let alone a diagnosis. Still, we wait. But they are drawing blanks. None of them know what has happened, and their next step is to defer to the brain injury specialists at the Walton Centre for Neurology and Neurosurgery in Liverpool.

I watch again as the doctors and nurses glide from bed to bed, their eyes scrolling down their clipboards as they make their first ward round of the day. 'Next job, Kerry,' they say, 'is to call the Walton and see if there's a bed for you.' As always, the answer is no. 'We'll ring back later,' the nurses say hopefully, as they break the news to me all over again.

'That's the lady waiting to go to the Walton,' they say to each other at handover, nodding across to me.

In the meantime, my mind bloats and swims with unanswered questions. I have never been someone who can cope with feeling out of control. I like repetition, structure and answers. My mind feels sluggish and slow, but through the fog I pick over my memories once more and try to make sense of it all again. I hadn't had a drink. I hadn't even been feeling unwell. I'd been sat in the lounge five minutes earlier, ready to see in the weekend. Had I missed something? Had Kings, whose own mind had blanked out parts of my ordeal, forgotten something crucial? Why did I feel like the doctors were ignoring us? And – most crucially – why couldn't I use my right arm? Why couldn't I feel anything down my right side?

Whatever this was – and we'd been left in the dark for so long that I was starting to fear it might be life-changing – had happened in a blink of an eye. How could life go wrong that quickly?

'The feeling will come back,' my family reassure me when they visit each day. 'That can happen after a stroke, can't it? Things heal again.'

After two days, a consultant visits from the Walton Centre to run some more tests. He checks my reflexes, my sight, asks me to raise and lower my arms.

'Can you feel anything?' he presses. 'Is the movement coming back?'

After five days, we have the green light to move to the Walton Centre. I am housed in a specialist brain injury ward. In the beds opposite are patients with cerebral palsy and a young man who has been in a car accident. His head is shaved on one side, revealing a scar dividing his scalp, which is punctuated with staples.

In this airy, open-plan ward, things feel more purposeful. I undergo more tests and scans. There is reassurance in knowing that this is the place that will finally give us answers, but as the days go on, I grow anxious at the rising stakes. *I'm so thankful*, I think, *for the life I have lived: that I was able to walk down the aisle, that I was able to have Casey. I'm so thankful that whatever this is has happened in adulthood, that my parents didn't have to face this when I was a child.*

That gratitude feels so vivid. At other times, it feels like we are in a dream.

• • •

'Is someone coming in for you today?' a nurse asks. I have been moved from the main ward into a side room with two other patients. It is the first ward round of the day.

'Yes,' I reply. 'Kings is coming in for afternoon visiting hours, as always.'

'Good,' she says. 'The consultant will be here and wants to have a conversation.'

*This is it, then*, I think. Every other day, they'd just tell me their plans for the latest round of tests. This is different. The tests have found something.

Pure dread pools in my stomach. What will they tell us? What have they found? What will life look like? Over the past four days, I've exhausted myself with unanswered questions, but now it feels like I'm dangling on the edge of a precipice, about to roll off. I think back over what answers we do have: a stroke. I'd had some sort of stroke.

• • •

The consultant is a greying, eccentric man dressed in a dicky bow and tweed jacket. Briskly, he ushers Kings and me into his office. I look at its sparse, whitewashed walls. There are no pictures, no diagrams or posters. He settles on one side of his desk and gestures for us to sit opposite.

'Right,' he begins, 'we now know what's happened.' There is no pause, no preamble. No indication that what he is about to say next will change our lives forever.

'You've had a cerebral bleed,' he says. 'The areas of your brain already damaged at birth have been attacked. In my opinion, you will never be able to walk again – the damage is irreversible. You will be paralysed for the rest of your life down the right side of your body.'

Our world falls apart.

I feel Kings put his arm across my shoulder and tears pool in my eyes. I look at the blank, bare walls. How fitting for our new life – for starting all over again.

'You have been lucky,' he continues. 'What happened should have killed you outright. It's far more common for that to happen than for people to be left as you have been.'

The words wash over me as tears speckle my cheek. Permanent headaches. Failing memory. No bladder and bowel control. Catheters. In the panic, my mind clings to the words 'irreversible damage' and plays them over and over again. My heart sinks further each time, crushed by how final they sound. I could have regained sensation after a stroke, even if only slightly. There is no coming back from this.

I watch as the consultant sifts through scans of my brain. His finger slides over the masses of grey to a perfect black circle. There's nothing there, I realise, but damage. There is no chance of learning to walk again. Whatever was there will never grow back.

'Do you have any questions?'

Kings and I sit in silence, tears pooling in our eyes. We don't know what questions to ask – or maybe we just have too many. Maybe we will hear answers we don't want to. How are we supposed to feel? Amid this complete, utter devastation, how are we supposed to deal with anything? We had never been warned that the outcome could be this bad. There had been no run-up, no time to prepare. We didn't know anything like this was on the cards until the moment we entered his office.

'I will give you some space,' the consultant says, pushing his chair back from the desk and walking stiffly to the door.

As Kings wheels me to the ward, I torment myself with the impact of all this on him. For starters, our house is an hour from Walton, and Kings has to drive there and back. That's two hours of his day taken up just on the roads, before you add in the actual visiting hours.

And what about the impact on his day-to-day life, once we're home? I had got married at twenty-seven and now, at thirty, I will need him to be my full-time carer. Kings didn't sign up for this, or whatever my – our – life will look like now. I think back to my thirtieth birthday party barely a month ago, and the room of hundreds of people that had danced the night away at the social club. That was our life, not this.

I don't want to hold Kings back, stop him from living a better life without me. I don't want him to stay with me out of pity. Are we going to last? Will he stay? And what will happen if he dies before me? I'm now totally dependent on him. I will never be able to manage on my own again. Without Kings, I'll have to go into a home.

My biggest worry is losing Casey. When I go home, I won't have any answers for her. I'd heard, as we all had, about what happens when social services become involved in a family, as they no doubt would with ours given our changed circumstances. What would happen if they thought that I couldn't care for Casey or be a mum? Surely, I'd have to provide evidence for everything, show them that I could cook and clean and iron her school uniform. Without my right arm, how would I be able to demonstrate any of that? What if they wrote me off? What if they thought me incapable? What if I actually was?

These thoughts are still swimming in my head as Kings pushes my wheelchair up our drive at home. When I'd first entered a wheelchair at the hospital, I had assumed it was temporary. Now, I am being steered into a different life. My heart sinks when I see the step to the front door: I feel Kings tilt my chair backwards and the front wheels roll over the lip.

As we come through the front door, I glance across to the kitchen and note for the first time the angle of the cupboards. My chair will not fit through. Kings and I look at each other. How will we navigate life when I can't do anything? How will we pick ourselves up from here?

The only place the chair will fit is our lounge, which has double doors that open up to what some families might use as a dining room. Kings has moved a bed down there for me. From now on, he will wheel me to and from my new bedroom to the lounge.

He can't, though, relocate the whole bathroom. A taxi will come twice a week, with a carer, to take me to a care home so that I can be hoisted into a bath. Outside of that, I'll have bed baths, and four visits a day from carers who will prepare my meals, dress me and put me back to bed each evening.

That care had come at the insistence of the social worker whose words continued to swirl in my head. 'This scenario splits families up,' he'd warned us. 'People don't stay together after things like this.'

He had said it so calmly, was so matter of fact about it all. Clearly, he didn't realise that he was burdening me with yet another insecurity. I play his words over and over, to the point where I go to sleep each night and think: *We've made it through another day.*

• • •

The thinking had been that four carers would take some pressure off Kings, but Kings still had to give up work to look after me. The carers also served to make me feel like I was a burden, not only incapable of looking after my family but needing scores of strangers to sweep in and out of the house each week.

Those same anxieties from the hospital resurfaced again and again: *What was Kings getting out of all this?* I didn't want him to stay with me as my carer; I wanted him to stay with me because he was my husband. I would have broken things off with Kings if I felt that he was only with me out of pity, even if I couldn't cope without him. He needed to want to be with me to make our marriage work.

'This is just our situation,' Kings would say to me constantly. 'It's not going to change. I'm not going away. You're still Kerry – just sitting down and not standing up.'

I struggled, though, with my new and sudden vulnerability. I had to have help with things that I didn't want anybody, let alone my husband, to see. I felt saddened that Kings was now my carer before he was my husband. Everything was about helping me, changing me, cleaning me. He told me that he didn't mind, but I already had carers in my life. I didn't want Kings to be one; I wanted him to be my husband.

When carers hoisted me to bed and announced they would be washing me, I told them to keep the bedroom door open. I didn't want to keep myself and my needs hidden from Kings and, most of all, Casey: to do so would make things secretive, shameful, a far bigger deal than they needed to be. That approach isn't for everyone, but I wanted Casey to see what was going on instead of building things up in her head.

It was almost like being a baby again because I couldn't do so many things for myself. Everything about our life before had changed.

However, it got to the point where Casey would look forward to particular carers coming to the house. She would want to tell them the latest chapter of whatever had been going on for her at school. She was unbothered about whatever they were working on and just wanted to be part of all the conversations. Over time, many of those carers have become family friends.

Casey and Kings would watch my sessions with the two physio-therapists who came to our house once a week. I would hang across a standing frame while they asked me to stand on my right leg. 'I can't,' I'd say, 'because then there'd be nothing holding me up.' My left leg, always the stronger of the two, was still working but I still had no feeling in my right. The physio's attempts to stimulate any kind of movement hadn't worked.

Losing yourself, I'd learn, is a gradual thing. It happens slowly, then you wake up one day and wonder where all the pieces of yourself went. Certainly, for the first twelve months, as a family we grieved as though I'd died. The Kerry we'd had before wasn't there anymore. As a kid, I had always been the loud, confident one with too much to say. In her place, we had this very different, anxious and insecure person who couldn't do anything. Everything was malfunctioning. Everything was wrong. I was embarrassed.

I didn't want to see people, for anyone to see how I looked now. Inevitably, I had put on weight, and I refused to have my picture taken or look in a mirror. Out shopping, I would make Kings change direction and wheel me down a side street if we saw someone I knew. I was hung up over what I perceived as a droop on the right-hand side of my face, ignoring Mum's insistence that she'd never noticed it before. In passing, some friends would offer platitudes – 'this hasn't changed who you are' – but those same friends were often those that stopped meeting with us. I lost countless friends because they couldn't deal with what happened to me – not just because I couldn't.

Joanne was one of the only people who didn't treat me any differently. Perhaps that's a result of her matter-of-fact nature; maybe she is just as loyal as I knew she would be. My friend Justine, who I've known since my teen years working shifts at the garage in Gwersyllt, also remained in my life. I treasure my relationship with her, and with her husband Allan, and we speak or message every day. Justine asked me to be maid of honour at her wedding – the only time I've ever been asked to do that – when I was, unbeknownst to us all, pregnant with Casey.

Members of the public were not so understanding. Strangers would turn away in shops or talk over me, like I didn't exist, and speak only to Kings. On a trip to a supermarket, one woman pushed out her bottom lip in pity every time we met her in the aisles. 'It's just so sad,' she'd say. 'You're so young.' It happened so many times that I asked Kings to skip the last few aisles just so we didn't have to see her again. People stared because they weren't used to seeing a young person in a wheelchair, but I didn't want people's pity.

There were periods where I felt so, so angry: why has this happened to us? Right before I was hospitalised, Kings and I had found a lender willing to help us buy our house and had been just a couple of weeks from the paperwork going through. Suddenly, we had no money. I was the first in my family to ever go on state benefits and the only one of my parents' children to not own their own house. Mum would wheel me around the supermarket: 'Get what you'd like,' she'd say, 'and I'll pay the bill.' But I didn't want to rely on other people's money.

Had we bought the house before the bleed, we wouldn't have been entitled to a penny in grants or assistance when it came to adapting it for my wheelchair. That our house was owned by the council meant we would have help, but it would be scant.

We had to fight tooth and nail for everything. When social services arrived to assess the house and me for an electric wheelchair, their first response was to turn me down – no matter that I couldn't use my right arm to wheel myself in a manual one, meaning Kings had to push me everywhere. They caved, but there would be an eighteen-month wait for the chair that would give me independence.

The biggest battle was for us to keep our home. Initially the council refused to work on our house. Prefabricated and built just after the war, they feared that it wasn't fit to adapt, and refused, at least five times, to widen the drive for the new van we would need so that I could get in and out of a vehicle with my chair. They wanted to move us to an already adapted property within the Wrexham borough.

I fought them with everything I had.

'Casey has had her whole life turned upside down,' I said. 'Her mum has gone into a wheelchair. I'm not moving her away from everything she's ever known – from a school she can walk herself to because she lives on that very road – and causing her more upheaval. This is her normal. She can't give up anything else.'

It was months of being deluged by emails as contractors and council workers paced through our rooms, scratched their heads and worked out what could be done. In the end, they said that they would not be able to build a lift upstairs to the bathroom, but could extend the back of the house to put one on the ground floor. It would take six to eight months, and we would have to live in the house while the work was going on.

I woke each morning to the noise of hammers, drills and the thought that would not leave me: *Is this my last day?*

In the hospital, the consultant had advised against an operation that would 'seal' the site of the bleed to prevent it from rupturing and bleeding again. In my case, the bleed was so deep and so entangled among nerve endings that there was a higher probability of me coming out of the surgery with further damage than there was of me waking up safely. My odds were less than fifty-fifty. As soon as I'd heard that, I'd agreed that I could not take the risk – not with Casey in my life.

I watched her play Mary in her nativity play and cried silently. *Will I see you next year?* I thought. *Will I see next Christmas?* Everything came with that disclaimer: this might be my last.

It's a cliché to say that kids are resilient, but it's true. In keeping everything as normal as possible for Casey, she was able to find joy in simply our presence at home – it was a novelty for her, as before we'd both been working and most of her friends were in the school breakfast and teatime clubs.

She noticed, though, that there were times when Kings and I seemed more easily stressed and frustrated. She didn't always understand why, beyond that I wasn't always well and that whatever had happened meant that we needed to make changes to the house. Kings and I were always quick to reassure her that everything was fine, that we were just tired that day, and she would go along with us, partly because it was easier for her to. She didn't want to dwell on the fact that things might not be OK for us.

Another lifeline was crafting, and I learned to hand-sew greetings cards. I would purchase a pattern, punch all the holes onto card in the marked places, thread a small needle with different colour threads and then sew the design. I found the process very therapeutic. It was quite an art, and the designs grew more intricate. I advertised them on Facebook and got orders from repeat customers. I was proud and honoured to do the wedding invitations for both my brothers' special days, for Ian's marriage to Lizzii and Matt's to Holly.

I embroidered Casey's name to go in her bedroom, too, and, as we hung it on the wall, I watched Casey with a mix of sadness and resolve. I still felt that I had so many reasons to live. I couldn't give up – for her.

# CHAPTER SIX

# *DRAGONHEART*

I never thought I'd be a football fan – never mind a Wrexham fan. That might seem strange when you consider who my dad is.

Dad began watching Wrexham as a youngster, from the old pen situated behind the goal and next to the old players' entrance. The first game he remembers was a 10–1 victory over Hartlepools United, as they were known at the time, in 1962, when he was eleven, in the season Wrexham were promoted to the Third Division (now called League One).

He told me stories: of a game against Liverpool at Anfield in the FA Cup in 1970, of promotions and of a Welsh cup win in Cardiff in 1972 that ended with a party at the team hotel. There were victories over Leicester City and Tottenham in the League Cup in 1976. He took trips across Europe to watch games against Porto, Roma, Zurich, Hajduk Split and Anderlecht. In 1981, Wrexham played West Ham in the FA Cup over three games – because there were no penalty shoot-outs in those days. Wrexham won that third match. He watched Wrexham become Third Division champions in 1978 with a 7–1 win over Rotherham. His favourite players were Mickey Thomas, Joey Jones, Billy Ashcroft, Bobby Shinton and Dixie McNeil.

Dad went to home and away matches for years. When he was in his twenties, he knew all of the players and he and his mates would sometimes travel on the first team bus with complimentary tickets for the matches. This was long before us kids were on the scene, at which point he stopped going to away matches until Ian was old enough to go with him.

Ian was a talented footballer, and Dad took over Ian's grassroots club, Caergwrle Wanderers, when it was at risk of folding. I would watch them on the occasional Sunday morning. When Ian, at sixteen, had to choose between going to drama school or taking up a place in what would have been the academy at Wrexham, he opted for the college place in London.

I can't claim that I was really invested in any of it. The horses took up so much of my time and I was always with Joanne. Football was my dad and Ian's domain. If I'm totally honest, I probably thought that football was a boy thing. I never watched football at home. I never felt a great hankering to be involved.

I went to the Racecourse only two or three times. I watched one game from the Kop stand: it was only half full, with enough space to run around when there was a lull in play, but it was the place to be for the singing and chanting. I still didn't have the bug by the time Wrexham went to the Millennium Stadium in Cardiff (Wembley was still under construction) for the 2005 Football League Trophy Final against Southend. I had to borrow a Wrexham top, but it was a balmy day and the atmosphere was out of this world. I'd never been anywhere like that. Fans had their faces painted, and I felt part of something as I watched the fans lapping up a final on Welsh soil. The pictures of my dad and me from that day are among my most treasured. But otherwise, I didn't leave matches wanting more.

Kings is the one who really got me into football. His relationship with Wrexham began in the 1980s – he thinks in '85 – and he fell in love with the club as he stood in the Kop with his mates. Games were so sparsely attended back then that he could pick out his dad standing in the other stand, and the stewards would let him move across to watch with his old man. Kings's dad then lost faith in the team and gave up, by which point Kings was a teenager and had started stewarding the away end.

He was working at a game against Arsenal in 1992 and still insists to this day that he helped save the life of the Arsenal manager, George Graham. At full time, Kings headed towards the tunnel as the late Tony Gubba was about to interview Graham for *Match of the Day*. Kings watched in horror as thirty Arsenal fans burst through the open Kop gate and began gesturing and shouting. Kings escorted Graham down the tunnel to safety. 'What would have happened if I hadn't?' Kings says. 'He'd have been mauled.'

Kings later took on all kinds of roles at the club. He grew up as a Liverpool fan, but Wrexham was his home team. His view was always that if he didn't buy a ticket to Anfield, the seat would still sell, but if he didn't get a ticket to Wrexham, the ground would stay empty. He sold Wrexham club lottery tickets and knocked on doors to collect money from a list of customers. He took Casey to a few games when she was little, but any football fan will know that your commitment to your club waxes and wanes depending on what else is going on in your life. There would be years when he didn't go, but his love of Wrexham was unconditional. That bond was always there. The love is never totally dormant.

In 2013, he signed up to host *Dragonheart*, Wrexham AFC's radio show, at the community radio station, Calon FM, based out of Glyndwr (now Wrexham) University. Spencer Harris had presented *Dragonheart* before he became a director of the club, but the show had since died off. However, advertisements began appearing looking for volunteers to revive it, and the university had state-of-the-art facilities for students who wanted to go into broadcasting and journalism.

Ten people turned up to the first meeting to re-establish the radio show, and they planned to run it on a rota. Kings had experience working on hospital radio, so they asked him to present the show while they all got their bearings. Over the following few weeks, though, as they realised the scale of the commitment – that it was more than just turning up for a chat about the game – volunteer numbers dwindled until *Dragonheart* was solely the domain of Kings and Andy, a fellow fan. Kings presented the show, collected interviews with staff and players, and edited all the audio. He had to be in the studio every week during the season and recorded a few episodes at the end of the campaign to sweep up any news. Then, he could take a deserved break in the off season.

The show was always recorded over two hours on a Thursday night and aired every Friday, but Kings found he was inundated with complaints from people who had missed it. He decided to work with the station to turn it into a podcast, which went out for the first time in 2016, paying a hosting company himself. It was then that the listening figures really took off.

It was an outlet for Kings, who had left his job to be my full-time carer. He enjoyed meeting players, interviewing managers and getting to see behind the scenes at the club, flexing all the privileges that fans don't usually get.

'I'm going down to the training ground,' he'd regularly say to me in the morning. 'Do you want to come for the ride?' The first few times, I stayed in the car. From where we were parked, I could watch training at Colliers Park and see Kings milling about with his recording equipment. He would return with tales about who he'd interviewed and what they'd said. Of course, I started to feel interested – dare I say it, I started to feel invested. I suppose it's a little bit like what happened when the world started to watch *Welcome to Wrexham*, but on a smaller scale: you get to know the key characters and their storylines, and you become part of something, eager to see what happens next. That Wrexham was a club owned and run by fans was also attractive to me. I was full of admiration for the dedication of a community that had come together to keep their football club alive.

The more time Kings spent at the club – he would be there at least twice a week – the more the Wrexham Supporters Trust chairman Pete Jones began to trust us. 'We're signing a new player tomorrow – do you want to come and interview him?' he'd say to Kings, who'd also get the heads up when a new manager was being appointed so that he could go to the press conference. The players respected the way Kings did things, so would give up their time to come into the radio studio to speak to him. Kings could walk around the club like he worked there. He was even awarded the Wrexham Supporters Trust Unsung Hero award at the end of the 2017/18 season.

Kings always behaved like he was part of the club's in-house media, so he never stitched up the people who had confided in him or barraged them with undue criticism. That was appreciated at that time when everybody – and I mean everybody – knew every bit of the club's business. Transfer dealings, bust-ups and staff changes were all reported to social media, and 90 per cent of the time the fans who claimed to be in the know were spot on.

The club might have been struggling in the National League, but behind the scenes, those were fun, easy-going, happy days. I felt so privileged to be a part of the players' lives, learning about their families, their interests, their problems. Being able to stand and talk to members of the board – faceless, shadowy figures at so many football clubs – was another big thing. I would compare our experience at Wrexham to Kings's with Liverpool, whose fans would never get this kind of opportunity to speak to all the players and know what was going on.

'If we're doing all this, I might as well go to a match,' I eventually said to Kings. Ahead of the 2014/15 season, that match became a season ticket. As we were on benefits, we couldn't afford to have things like that, but this was where Nan stepped in. We nicknamed her 'the money fairy' because three or four times a year she would put generous amounts of money in an envelope for each of her five grandchildren. The money always seemed to arrive when we needed it most, and year after year, the money she gave us in May paid for our season ticket. Without her, we'd never have been able to go to matches.

The Kop had closed in the late 2000s because it was so unsafe, but it was still standing. People were very sentimental about it even though it was derelict, with weeds growing through the cracks in the concrete and between the rows of sun-bleached barriers that fans had leant against in the days gone by. When the Kop was demolished in January 2023, the Trust repainted those barriers and sold them off so that people could buy them for their gardens. There's one outside the Turf pub that's often featured in *Welcome to Wrexham*.

The plan was always to rebuild a new, more glorious Kop, but there was never enough money. The stand behind the goal was just flat land, a fitting symbol for how so much history had been ripped out of one end of the club. The closure of the Kop, Kings thinks, had a big impact on the mood at matches because fans either drifted away from the team completely or moved to other parts of the ground. There was very little atmosphere then, with games only ever attended by a few thousand people at most. The diehard fans would make noise but nothing like what the crowds do now. I'm grateful I got to experience a match from the original Kop as a teenager, even if I didn't take it in at the time.

I grew to understand football. I felt the highs and the lows – so much so that, after the defeat by Eastleigh in the play-offs in 2019, I cried all the way from the gate to the car. From our vantage point on the front row, we felt part of the action. When Wrexham scored, we were all but on the pitch. If players ran to the stand behind us, they celebrated directly with us. As players set up to take throw-ins, they would turn and talk to us. Years later, in 2022, Ben Tozer, with whom we always got on brilliantly, said that he would dedicate a goal to us if he scored. When he did, he ran towards us and high-fived Kings – but missed me because I was lower down in my wheelchair! Still, we were pulled into the team celebration.

I was swept up by the elation and excitement of wins and found myself really looking forward to Saturdays so that I could go and be part of something. That season ticket meant friendship with the people on the surrounding rows. I fell more in love with the community we built and the story of this self-sustaining, fan-run club than I did the football on the pitch. There were so few fans that those of us who were there week in and week out built incredibly tight bonds and found a very powerful sense of camaraderie. We built a community, one in which people saw me for who I was, possibly for the first time in my life, and accepted me totally – wheelchair and all.

After the bleed, there were people who had vowed to keep in touch but stepped away. I lost scores and scores of friends who, for whatever reason, no longer wanted to be part of my life. That sense of being invisible permeates other aspects of life in a wheelchair. In early 2025, I was on a course about improving accessibility when the instructor played a video of a wheelchair user and their family member in the supermarket. Every time the checkout assistant spoke, it was to address the standing family member. Even when the person in the wheelchair replied and handed over the money, the staff member totally ignored them and handed the change to the person standing.

'Any comments?' the instructor asked.

I raised my hand. 'Welcome to my world.'

That's exactly how it is. People talk to Kings and expect that I can't speak or hold a conversation. It's not like that at the club. I wonder sometimes if fans even see the wheelchair. I feel like they don't. Perhaps that's because they've only ever known me with it. In any case, they accepted me instantly. They never turned away or didn't want to talk to me.

That's a poignant thing because throughout my life I'd never felt accepted. I was bullied at school. Then I finished school and ended up in an abusive relationship. I never felt worthy until people at Wrexham saw me for who I was. That meant more than people will ever understand.

## CHAPTER SEVEN

# 'WELCOME TO WREXHAM, KERRY EVANS'

Our trip to Macclesfield in 2016 made for one of our stand-out moments as Wrexham supporters. As we made our way through the separate gated entrance and to our place along the front row of the main stand, a man in a manual wheelchair introduced himself.

'I'm Andy,' he began, 'the disability liaison officer at Macclesfield. I'm here if you need anything. Do you know where the toilets are? Do you need a blanket? Have you been to Macclesfield before?' He showed us to our seats further along the stand and asked us how our journey had been. 'If you need anything during the game, I'll be sitting over there,' he said, pointing over his shoulder to the open segregation gate that separated the sets of fans. 'Just come and find me.'

We watched as he went up and down the stand, doing the same with every new arrival.

Kings and I were taken aback. No one had ever made us feel that welcome at an away game before. Usually you were left to your own devices, contending with subpar facilities, waiting for accessible toilets to be unlocked and having to explain to stewards what kind of provisions you needed. Here, someone had gone out of their way to welcome us to their club. Andy had not only made sure we were being looked after but had taken on that role himself.

At half time, Andy came back – with a plate of cupcakes in tow – to check how we were getting on and see how we'd found the match so far. The cupcakes had been left in the boardroom, so he offered them to us. As any away fan will tell you, that definitely isn't usual protocol.

I asked him about his role: what was a disability liaison officer (DLO), and why had we never come across one before? He wasn't employed by the club but volunteered solely on a matchday to meet and greet the away fans, show them how to find things and make them feel welcome.

'What you're doing is so lovely,' I said. 'You've made me feel so special. And the cake was a lovely touch. We've never come across this before. We've not been welcomed like this anywhere. It just doesn't happen.'

'I'm just a huge fan of the club,' he said. 'I wanted to be able to help.'

In the van that night, I turned to Kings. 'Wrexham need a DLO,' I said. 'That would be a great thing to have. Someone at Wrexham should give our visiting fans that feeling of being safe and included.'

When we returned to Wrexham, I reached out to WST chairman Pete Jones and told him about Andy and how much we valued the reception he'd given us.

At this point, I didn't know what a DLO was beyond the experience we'd had at Macclesfield. Andy hadn't talked of accessible tickets or a five-day working week, and I hadn't looked into jobs in football. My chat with Pete was solely about how someone had brought that human touch to our away trip. Pete acknowledged that it was a lovely thing, but we didn't have a broader discussion about accessibility at the club. I didn't know that anything more would come of our chat. When the club was under the control of the WST, those were the kind of lowkey conversations you'd have. I'd always be catching up with people while Kings was collecting material for *Dragonheart*.

The next we heard was when Kings's phone pinged while we were on a cruise to the Mediterranean. It was from Pete, letting us know that the club were now looking for a disability liaison officer of their own. They had advertised the role – voluntary, as was the way at the time – and the closing date was approaching.

'We would urge Kerry to apply,' Pete had written.

'They're going to do what Andy does at Macclesfield,' Kings said.

*I could do that*, I thought. Andy had been lovely and welcoming, and I thought I'd be capable of doing his kind of role. I'd be confident enough to tell people where the toilets were. It would give me something to do and be a break from just being at home all the time, where all the days can so easily blend into one without work. I welcomed the idea of structure and responsibility.

I went home and began pulling together a CV. Of course, I'd not worked since the cerebral bleed at thirty, so I was almost starting from scratch. I looked at the computer and worried whether, in Wrexham's eyes, my employment history would look sparse. I hadn't had many jobs, and I hadn't worked for about ten years by that time. I wrote a few sentences about going into a wheelchair so that the club would know why there were all those gaps.

Mostly, though, it felt strangely formal. Why did we have to fill out all of this paperwork – there were other application forms to look at, too – when this was just a voluntary role welcoming people on matchdays? Had Andy had to do all of this?

My interview was at 2 p.m. on a weekday. We pulled through the gates and into the front car park, and Kings waved me off to the double glass doors of the Club 1864 entrance. I shook with nerves.

The interview was held in the hospitality boxes in the Hays Travel stand. You could see the pitch through the glass window. I felt a quick sweep of adrenaline at being behind the scenes and going to a part of the club I'd never seen before. At one side of an oval table sat the stadium manager Phil Bennett and Colin Williams, an occupational psychologist by day and member of the board by night.

I wheeled myself to the other side and took them in. Phil wore a Wrexham hoodie, his elbows on the table, and was sitting so casually that I half-wondered if he was bored. Only Colin wore a suit. Maybe I should have taken Colin as a sign of how seriously the club were taking this.

'Why do you want to do this?' began Colin.

'I want to make a difference,' I started, recounting the story of Andy at Macclesfield. I explained why I'd been out of work for so long and what had happened to me after my cerebral bleed, that I would be able to understand what people were going through when they came to me with their problems, and that I'd love to feel like I had something to offer again.

'I want to make people feel welcome,' I concluded, feeling pleased with my first answer.

Then the interview shifted. Colin began reading through guidelines and legislation, asking me for my thoughts. My mind began to race as I realised I'd made one crucial error: I hadn't researched what a disability liaison officer actually was. I hadn't considered that it would be anything different from what Andy did. But Wrexham weren't looking for an Andy; they were looking for somebody to take on – unpaid – a full-time job role within the club. That simply wasn't what I'd gone in for.

It hit me like a slap in the face, and I could almost feel the breath being driven from my body. This was a million miles from the role I'd created in my head, of someone who was just going to welcome and chat with the home and away fans.

Two minutes. That's all it had taken before I was foolishly, hopelessly out of my depth. I felt my face flush as Colin tied me up in knots. *How silly and naive he must find me*, I thought. I would never have gone to the interview if I'd known what they were really after. I was kicking myself that my ignorance had got me into this situation.

Phil, meanwhile, said nothing as Colin continued, rapid fire and without pause, to move down the list of stadium requirements. As someone who hadn't worked for years and had never been involved in football, I felt like I couldn't keep up with him. At the same time, he still gave the impression that his every word had been carefully weighed and chosen. I shrank in the face of his clear intelligence.

'I'm sorry,' I said glumly. 'I just don't know how to answer that.' I tried not to let it show, but I grew more and more worked up inside. All the while, Phil never said a word. By the end of my ordeal I couldn't get out there quickly enough.

Kings watched me race towards the van. He could see, as he climbed down from the front seat, the tears well up in my eyes.

'We need to go,' I said. 'Just drive.'

Kings looked bewildered. What could have happened in that

forty minutes for me to leave in such distress? I'd gone in nervous but willing to give it my best shot. How could it have unravelled this badly?

'It can't have been that awful,' he replied. 'What have they said?'

'This is the thing!' I said, utterly flustered. 'I can't even remember to tell you. I can't believe I've just made an absolute fool of myself.'

'No, you didn't.'

'No, Kings! You weren't there. I *did* make a fool of myself. I didn't know any of the answers, and I didn't know what I was talking about. They're not looking for what you and I thought this job was going to be. I can't believe I even went for that.'

'Don't be silly. You won't have done that badly,' Kings continued, trying to both console me and get to the bottom of it all. 'Just forget about this, Kerry. In a few days, it will all be behind you.' Kings knows I'm an overthinker, that I can take the smallest things and still be stewing over them hours later. And those are for small things. For a big thing like this interview, he was aware it had the potential to really knock me back.

What made it worse was that these were people that we – Kings, especially – had known for years at Wrexham. I'd indirectly embarrassed him in front of his colleagues, all of whom had watched me turn into a laughing stock because I'd underestimated the role and gone in without having done any research. *Why did they ask that? What did I say that for? What answer did I give then?* I replayed every moment with a sinking sense of horror in my stomach. Those people run a football club! And there I'd been, thinking I could just turn up without any preparation!

Two days later, outside the Post Office, I received the call from an unknown number that would change my life.

'Is that Kerry Evans?'

'Yes. Hi.'

'It's Colin Williams from Wrexham AFC.'

I swallowed. I knew what was coming: 'Thank you, but you're not the right fit for us. Good luck in the future.'

'Just to let you know that we'd like to offer you the job.'

I shook my head with disbelief. 'Sorry?'

'We'd like to offer you the job.'

'You're joking.'

I heard a sharp intake of breath on the other line. 'Why would you think I was joking?'

I explained to Colin how I had made a fool of myself and embarrassed Kings in the process. Colin hadn't seen it that way. 'You were the outstanding candidate,' he said. 'We knew straight away that we wanted to offer you the job role.'

I've found out since that I was the only disabled person who applied for the role. I think that's a key part of why I've become so good at my job. I understand what people are going through because I'm living it. It doesn't matter how well-qualified you are: if you're not in that situation, you can't know the reality of it like I can. It was very forward-thinking of the club.

In the first few months of 2017, I started my new job under Colin's guidance. We would meet weekly at the Centenary Club. Wrexham had never had a disability liaison officer before, but Colin had a very clear idea of what he wanted the role to look like. To begin with, I would go in for two or three hours twice a week. We talked through what he expected of me and what I'd need to learn, and he would send me away with homework to follow up on. I didn't keep full-time hours but I had to be at the club on matchdays and work in my own time to affect the changes we needed.

I was introduced to the Sports Grounds Safety Authority, the UK government's adviser, and their Guide to Safety at Sports Grounds (Green Guide). At over a thousand pages, it covers more than you can imagine: accessible toilets, gradients of ramps, widths of doors, heights of counters, chevrons, markings, sight lines, ambulant-disabled seats versus disabled seats. It wasn't compulsory for National League clubs to meet all these requirements, but I'll always be proud that we aimed for English Football League standards even when we didn't need to.

I have enormous respect for Colin. He is a supremely clever man, but his intelligence intimidated me and I felt like I couldn't ever keep up. Even as the so-called outstanding candidate, I felt incapable and was overwhelmed by the volume of information that he would throw at me and everything I'd taken on. I suffered massively with imposter syndrome and my thoughts were all negative. He dissected what I felt were simple questions into granular detail and only stopped once we'd run through every eventuality. It was an excellent grounding for the role I've built for myself but not the easiest thing for someone reacquainting themselves with the workplace and low on confidence after ten years out!

Colin's view was that I didn't understand what I was capable of. 'You're good enough to do this job,' he said. 'Your self-esteem is absolutely shattered. All you need is confidence. You've just got to believe in yourself.'

He would run me through the things that were already in place at the Racecourse and then we'd move on to what I needed to start working on. I drew on that early experience at Macclesfield and contacted the club so that they could pass on my number to Andy. When he called, I told him that the reason I'd got the job at Wrexham was because of him and how he'd made us feel that day. He'd already given me lots of ideas for matchdays.

'They had blankets at Macclesfield – maybe we could give those out to wheelchair users,' I suggested to Colin. The blankets, along with wheelchair ponchos, were the first things I introduced as DLO. I received a donation for the ponchos from a local embroidery company called Top Marks, who purchased twelve at about £30 each.

That introduced me to another key aspect of the job: fundraising and networking. When I got the job, I hadn't been given a budget. In fact, I'd been told that if I wanted anything, I'd have to find the money myself. I wasn't alarmed by that because it was just the Wrexham way – we were a fan-owned club with no money to spare. I had to make the club more inclusive, but there wouldn't be a penny to do it with.

Looking back, that was a huge thing to carry on my shoulders. How can you make a difference without any money? But my message to clubs who think that they don't have the budget to improve access is that some of the things I've implemented at Wrexham didn't need that much funding. Occasionally, I think what holds clubs back is a lack of knowledge: they haven't put the thought into what they might need to do to help certain groups. Our red blankets cost £3 each. Making toilets stoma-friendly – as you'll later learn – is easy. I was lucky to have skilled fans able to help with some renovations, but I was also using the little money I did have wisely. The first items in our sensory room were fidget spinners I'd found for £1.99 each and donations of good-quality books. Initially, I worked exclusively with the small amounts of money that people donated to fund anything that needed doing.

In 2015, the Disabled Supporters Association (DSA), in conjunction with the club and Glyndwr University, had installed a platform at height in the Hays Travel stand (which is now known as the Macron stand) to allow six wheelchair users and their companions to watch the game. That was already an improvement on the clubs whose accessible spaces are at the front of stands, leaving wheelchair users exposed to the worst of the weather. Beyond that, however, there was very little in place when it came to accessibility and inclusion. The club had brought me in to find ways to welcome new fans, so I had to start thinking about how exactly we'd do that.

I'm honest enough to admit that when I started the role, my priority was helping wheelchair users – because I am one, and that was what was familiar to me. Until I needed a wheelchair, I had never been around people with disabilities. I'd never even thought of myself as disabled. How could I have, when I walked down the aisle with Kings? And for those with little knowledge of disability, the first thing that will spring to mind is wheelchair users.

I lived in this little bubble that I was going to help wheelchair users come to watch the football at Wrexham. I laugh at that now because that is the most stereotypical, able-bodied view on disability. I have to admit, though, that it was *my* view on disability, even if it was a very narrow-minded view of who I was at the club to help and support.

When the role got underway properly, I realised that there were hidden disabilities. People used walkers. People used sticks. We had autistic fans, fans with sensory issues, blind fans, deaf fans, fans living with dementia. The more you do, the more work you realise there is to be done. My fundraising would grow more ambitious to pay for hearing loops and money for braille signage.

*How did I get from wanting to be Wrexham's Andy – welcoming people to the club – to what I've taken on?* If I had a pound for every time I'd thought that during my time at Wrexham, I wouldn't need to work there because I'd be a millionaire. The job wasn't what I expected, but from the outset it brought me so much more fulfilment than I ever thought possible.

Having the trust of the football club brought me confidence, but this was always more to me than a job. It was an opportunity. It was a chance to change my life, in a way: to give me a purpose again, to give me something to get up for every day. I've always felt I owe Wrexham a great debt for handing me this lifeline. I wanted to make Colin proud and repay his early faith in me.

My parents and Kings definitely noticed a difference in me. I've always thrown myself into things and been an all-or-nothing person, and it was the same with this role. Before, when I wasn't working, I had kept busy – interested in life – with little projects and passions. Casey remembers my marine life phase, which involved us buying huge fish tanks and me signing up to scores of Facebook groups to ask experts for advice. She trudged behind me in tropical fish shops, growing bored as I interrogated the owners. That's why Casey didn't think much of my volunteering at Wrexham initially: she thought it was just another thing I'd taken on to keep me busy, even though she accepted that getting out regularly to meet people was a big thing. She never thought of me as less of a mum, less of a person or less capable while I wasn't working – in contrast to how I'd often seen myself during that period.

But Casey acknowledges that the child she was back then wasn't always able to grasp just how far out of my comfort zone the DLO role was for me. Only as she's grown older has she been able to understand that.

I knew that any decision I would make would have a real impact on people. Fans would come to me and say that, without the changes I put in place, they wouldn't have been able to come to a game. It's a privilege to have that impact on people's lives. I was popular with away fans, too, who remarked that no one from the home club had ever come over to check on them during the game until they'd been to Wrexham and met me. I'd think back to Andy, who had started it all. The way he had made me feel was exactly the impact I want to have at Wrexham.

It's rare in a football club to find someone who never has the difficulty of making unpopular decisions. Mine are always about improving access and making things better. I've always said that if there's a reason that somebody can't come to Wrexham AFC, I want them to tell me. I can't put things right if I don't realise what the problem is. If I can get something in place to make their life better, I will. The personal touch is really important at Wrexham and to my role especially. People confide in me and tell me of their troubles because they feel that they can trust me.

Within just six months, the job became an all-consuming thing, and my hours were full-time or thereabouts. In other ways, though, my voluntary role came with far more freedom than convention-al employment. If I wanted to go on holiday, I could just take two weeks off and didn't need to clear it with anybody.

I didn't do anything without Colin by my side in those early days, but it would soon all be down to me. What projects did I want to take on next and how would I make a difference?

# CHAPTER EIGHT

# KERRY'S RED BLANKETS

In my role as disability liaison officer, I've always been a voice for disabled fans. They came to me with their questions and suggestions – but nobody actually asked for accessible away travel. I think that's because no one ever thought it would be possible.

Non-disabled fans have travelled with Pat's Coaches for the entire time I've been at the club. There might be ten club coaches going to one game, but before 2018 there was nothing in place for wheelchair users. If they wanted to go to an away game, they had to get themselves there, and it was obvious to me that we would have lots of supporters who wouldn't be able to do that.

Since the takeover, the club has become known for its sold-out home matches and the great atmosphere at the Racecourse, but any football fan who's had the opportunity to go to an away match will know that there's something different about them. Being on the road brings a carnival atmosphere. You feel part of something – part of a community and a culture. The hardened fans who follow the team up and down the country all develop friendships with each other. It was only fair that wheelchair users could attend away games, too.

The club was short of office space and its boardroom was up two flights of stairs, so any meetings I attended were held in the Centenary Club, a hospitality area within the stadium that, crucially for me, is all on one level. When I decided to take my proposal for accessible travel provision to the board in early 2018, I went into that meeting knowing that I wouldn't get the money I needed for the scheme. No way. My hope was just to get permission to raise the funds.

I outlined my idea and a rough estimation of how much we'd need: £3,500. The feeling among the club was that I was trying to do the impossible – that there was no way I'd be able to find that kind of money. They acknowledged that I'd done so much, but that this was a bridge too far. The club didn't have money. I didn't have money.

The club learned very quickly, however, that I've never been good at taking no for an answer. I'll always come back to them with a solution or another way of doing something.

'Well, if I can raise the money,' I said, 'and personally take charge of all the fundraising, could we then run it? Would you let me go ahead with that?' The reply came: 'Yes, of course.'

I knew this round of fundraising would need to be more ambitious than any I'd done before. A quiz night might bring in £150, but that wouldn't touch the sides. Kings and I were always bouncing ideas off each other. I'm a horrendous sleeper and do lots of my thinking at night, my mind churning through ideas.

Finding the money was only half the story. Finding a suitable travel company was almost impossible. Every single one gave the same responses: they either didn't have accessible coaches, or they were too far away to help us and would charge us a fortune just to get to Wrexham. In desperation, I called companies as far as Runcorn, a forty-minute drive from Wrexham, and with each rejection I felt my heart sink. I knew we'd be able to raise the money – Wrexham fans had always rallied behind me, knowing the good my work did – but I had no idea just how hard it would be to find a bus.

Maybe I shouldn't have been surprised. Even now, in 2025, so much support is lacking for wheelchair users. Where it is available, it can be charged at a premium. I look back now and think: *No wonder I was still drawing blanks after four months.*

Clubs in the English Football League weren't even providing this kind of service. I know because I contacted lots of them asking which coach provider they used. The rote reply was: 'We don't run anything like that.'

One company was able to help us: Valentine Travel Solutions. They had wheelchair-adapted minibuses, mainly for school contracts during the week. The owner, Chris, was fully behind us and promised to run the service as cheaply as he could. But cheap still meant a phenomenal difference from the cost of Pat's Coaches. They might charge £12.50 per fan to travel for a match nearby – forty-eight people on each bus soon keeps the cost down – or maybe £25 for a fixture to London. We wanted to match Pat's prices for each wheelchair passenger and have their companions travel free of charge, but our bill for each minibus trip was reaching £400 for local away matches, up to £600 if it was in London, and we could only transport four wheelchairs at a time. We were essentially paying for a taxi service.

£3,500 would get us seven trips, and only to the closest fixtures, that first season. You can see, then, why we needed to think big.

Kings and I had always brought our own blankets to matches. One of my first acts as DLO had been to purchase a batch of red blankets to offer to wheelchair users (grey blankets for the away fans – I'm not sure they'd have thanked me if I'd given them one in Wrexham colours!) for night matches and winter Saturdays.

One of the effects of my cerebral bleed is that the right side of my body cannot regulate temperature. Even without this complication, it's so much colder sitting in a wheelchair than sitting in a regular seat huddled amid rows of fans and their body heat. If you're paralysed, you can't jiggle your legs or rub your arms to keep warm. So many wheelchair users would tell me how grateful they were for the blankets we provided.

I knew we were on to something.

A red blanket is one thing, but how could I make them Wrexham's? Macron, the club's kit supplier, agreed to embroider the badges – with a catch. The blankets came individually wrapped. They'd have to pay their staff to take every blanket out the wrapper, undo the tie around the middle, embroider the Wrexham badge and package them back up. We struck a deal: if Kings and I would open and repackage them, they'd embroider the crest at a cut price of £1.50.

I went online and began pricing things up. The blankets would cost £3, and, after Macron did their bit, if I sold them for £10 a pop, I'd be making a £5.50 profit on each blanket.

I got the go-ahead from Geoff Scott, Wrexham's commercial manager at the time, to test the waters with fifty blankets. The club would loan me the money, but they couldn't stock them in the club shop. The shop wasn't what it is now, full of lots of staff fulfilling orders from all over the world. It was so tiny that its managers back then had to be conscious of how much space each item took up. They just wouldn't have had the room for the hundreds of blankets I'd need to shift to raise the money I needed. This was on me.

Within weeks, boxes filled our hallway. One sofa was buried beneath our stock, the blankets rolled up like sausages and stacked seven high. We set up the ironing board as a makeshift packing station to keep the material flat. And on we went, slashing through the cellophane, folding and stacking the blankets into boxes for Macron and keeping the plastic safe to wrap everything up like new again.

Casey thought we had lost the plot. 'Don't even ask,' she'd say to the friends she had over as they shimmied their way past the boxes and bubble wrap. 'I'm going upstairs.'

Kings would stack the blankets in the car – helpfully, Macron's factory was on an industrial estate only two and a half miles from our house – and drive them to their door. Two or three days later, we'd get a call: 'We need the space. You need to come and collect your blankets right away.' Off Kings went, and then we'd be on the living room floor again, rolling them back up into the cellophane, slipping in the card with the manufacturing details and taping the bag back up.

I was confident we'd be able to shift the first fifty and that I'd be able to put the profit into buying more blankets. I put word out at the club and on Facebook and a wave of support had built before our first batch had even gone on sale. I took pre-orders and Kings and I waited outside Gate 12 with a pen and paper crossing customers' names off our list.

Then it really took off. I told Kings we'd have to order another hundred and do it all over again: the unpacking, the delivery, the collection and the repacking. Part of him went: 'Really? We're doing this again?' I always say that the ideas come from me, and Kings just gets dragged along for the ride. But he was always on board, as he is with all my plans. He had gone to lots of away games in his life and admitted that he'd always taken getting there for granted. He knew this was a great idea and wanted to give other people that joy he'd had at matches.

After a couple of weeks, the boxes would disappear from the front room because we'd sold out once more. And then we'd order another hundred. I'd post the pictures of our furniture drowning in boxes and blankets on Facebook. 'Kerry's red blanket factory is back up and running!' I'd write. 'We've got another hundred. We're going to be outside Gate 12 on Saturday.'

That's how it was, for weeks and months. When it rained, we'd be there with umbrellas. We'd sell out and Kings would have to run back to the car for more stock. People would come back week after week to buy more for their friends and family. All these years later, I still see people going through the turnstiles with their red blankets tucked under their arms.

It's funny to look back on it. Would Wrexham AFC, now as professional as it is, allow me these days to sell blankets at a market stall outside the accessible entrance? No way! But back then the WST let me get on with it.

Selling those blankets became everything to me. 'Campaign' doesn't feel like the right word, but people were swept along with me. The commercial manager at the club shop said to me at one point that they would never have been able to shift them like Kings and I did: Kerry's red blankets had a real story and heart. Other clubs got in touch with us to ask us how I'd done it all, where the blankets were from and whether they did other colours.

One of the more surreal bits of promotion I did was appear on Kings's *Dragonheart* podcast for a thirty-minute interview. I describe it as surreal because the minute the microphones went live, he went into professional mode. It was like he didn't even know me. For the next half an hour, he interviewed me as he would anybody else, before sheepishly ending with: 'Well, for anybody who doesn't know, Kerry is actually my wife.'

Other than that, though, I didn't do much marketing – it all grew very organically. That's how things used to be at Wrexham in the years before Ryan and Rob came on board: we had no money, we made do and mended, and people threw their support behind each other. In fact, of all the good times at Wrexham, the blankets era ranks as a real high for me. Over three seasons, we packed, repacked and sold 680 of them. Together with sponsorship money, donations from supporter groups, nearly £1,500 just from a bucket collection, passenger costs and other fundraising activities, we were able to put on an unprecedented travel service for our disabled fans. It's very humbling to think that people are buying into what you're trying to do.

Our first trip to an away match, against Solihull Moors on 27 August 2018, was an ecstatic moment: we had done it! One man in his twenties went to home matches with his mum but had never been to an away game. Another passenger had a sandwich and a packet of crisps to last him the 168-mile round trip (he now brings a picnic with him each time). Somebody else hadn't been to an away game for more than ten years. Grown men were in tears because of how much it meant to them to be able to watch Wrexham away. Despite the emotion, fans quickly named us the fun bus.

I was so proud of what we'd achieved. I took £16 from each of the four passengers and their companions travelled for free, just as we had wanted. The bus cost £200, and the shortfall was covered by the money we'd raised. All of our efforts had finally paid off.

Often, we stopped at a service station on the way, which could be complicated. Where Pat's passengers would just file off the coach, our driver would have to come and undo the four clips that anchored every wheel as well as the seatbelts that plugged into the floor. En route to Leyton Orient, Pat's coaches pulled up alongside us as our passengers were disembarking. We could hear the Wrexham chants floating from outside and everyone on the fun bus joined in. That was when it hit me: *this is special.* It was the first time I realised what a big achievement this was. Because those people around me were part of something – and that wouldn't have happened if it wasn't for me.

In the first year, Wrexham lost every game the fun bus travelled to – it became a running joke. My blanket customers would stop me at the ground: '*Please* tell us you're not coming to the game this weekend!'

The only drawback to those away matches was that National League-level grounds weren't the easiest places for wheelchair users to navigate, and the clubs struggled to accommodate us.

For the scheme's first three seasons, I worked as a steward on the bus and I saw it all. Ninety per cent of the time, away supporters in wheelchairs would be sat with the home fans and most likely be in a corner somewhere – the view wasn't always the best. One ground didn't have a ramp for their accessible toilet; one didn't even have an accessible toilet! When they did, they were often horrendous spaces. We would ask stewards for directions and they wouldn't know how to help us. Very few clubs had their own DLO on hand to help. More training was needed.

At Altrincham, the wheelchair seats were in a bus shelter-style structure, with the pitch on the other side of the glass. The windows were so dirty that we couldn't see the pitch, and it was even worse when it was raining. We would joke that we'd have to start taking our own Shammy cloths and bucket to wash it down. That structure was only a couple of feet away from the pitch so it would have offered a great view – if we'd been able to see anything.

We arrived at Barrow to find a six-inch step blocking the way to my seat. 'Don't worry,' a steward said. 'We'll go and get the ramp.' He returned a few minutes later. 'So, we can't find the ramp,' he said. 'But don't worry! We'll get you there another way.'

The other way was back out the stand, down the road, through another entrance, across the entire length of another stand, across the pitch, past the dugouts, past the managers and players and along to our seats. If we wanted to go to the toilet, we would have to go all the way back across the dugout: imagine the managers deep in thought about tactics and team selection suddenly seeing me trundling past! It was ridiculous. As it happened, the manager stepped out from the dugout at the final whistle just as we were trying to get past him.

My response to that kind of inconvenience has always been to just laugh about it. A few years ago, when we knew the managers and the players, that kind of thing was less of an issue. Now that everything is more professional, I might feel a bit more self-conscious, but I'd like to think I wouldn't encounter that particular problem higher up the divisions.

Later that year, I found out I'd been nominated for the inaugural 2018 National Game Community Award by the Football Supporters' Federation (now Football Supporters' Association), which represents more than half a million football fans throughout the pyramid. The category I was entered into was to recognise everything that non-league clubs did to keep the game going outside the top four leagues, and Wrexham had received a nomination because of my work with disabled supporters. The club wanted to send me to the ceremony at the Tower of London in December.

My instinct was to turn them down. Given we were on benefits, we just couldn't afford to go. It was right before Christmas and there were gifts to buy. We couldn't afford the hotel; I couldn't even afford the new top I'd need. Nan insisted I had to go and paid for everything. That's what she was like: extraordinarily generous. When Casey was a toddler, for example, Nan and Granddad started the annual tradition of taking the whole of my mum's side of the family away on holiday, even handing out envelopes of spending money to each of us. As our family expanded, the initial party of eleven became twenty, and we would joke that any new partners had to stand on the end of pictures so that we could cut them out if the relationship didn't work out. Mum and Uncle Glyn have kept this going since Nan's passing.

We arrived to a who's who of football: Kings pointed out Gary Neville and Martin Tyler in one corner. It all felt so beyond me. I'd just been a volunteer at a club – a completely normal person who just happened to find something I loved and a passion. How had we got to this point? I was just little old Kerry in a wheelchair.

I became known that night as 'Kerry red blankets', firstly by Lincoln City's supporter liaison officer Alan Long and then Robbie Savage, Wrexham born and bred. 'You're Kerry red blankets!' he boomed as we had a photo together.

Throughout the season, volunteers at National League clubs had also been recognised with the Volunteer of the Month awards. I'd won in September 2018 and was presented with my award by the first-team player Akil Wright out on the pitch.

Unbeknownst to me, each month's winner had been put in for another award.

Kings and I were driving into town when the call came in from Spencer Harris. I told Kings to pull over and we ended up on double yellow lines. Spencer wanted to invite me to the National League's AGM, which would involve an overnight stay at the five-star Celtic Manor Resort in Coldra Wood in Newport.

'Well, how much will cost?' I asked. Back then, an overnight stay for Wrexham meant funding it yourself. You'd think that directors would get expenses, but every year that Spencer was a director at the club, he paid for his own season ticket.

'No – we have to pay for this,' Spencer said. 'Each National League club has a table and we have to bring a certain number of volunteers from the club. We'd like you and Kings to come as guests. You'll have a fabulous night. It's to say thank you. You do such a fantastic job for the club.'

We drove down on Saturday morning and found ourselves in the fanciest hotel room I'd ever stayed in. In my experience, accessible rooms are always the most basic, but in this room we must have lost fifteen minutes just marvelling at the marble bathroom. Kings and I went to explore further when we were stopped by a stranger at the lift.

'Hi, Kerry! Lovely to meet you!' he said. He introduced himself as a National League staff member who was the master of ceremonies on the night. 'I've heard so much about you. Congratulations on your award!'

I frowned. 'Sorry?'

His face dropped. 'I… I'm so sorry!' He stuttered. 'You… You don't know, do you?'

I never told Spencer that his big surprise had been ruined. When I was announced as Volunteer of the Year out of all seventy-two clubs in the National League pyramid, I acted as shocked as everyone else around the table. Spencer, if you're reading this: I felt so guilty – sorry!

• • •

In the second season of hosting accessible away travel, we got a sponsor on board who gave us £1,000 of the £3,800 we needed.

W. B. Environmental was run by two brothers whose parents brought them to Wrexham matches as young boys. They got involved because away days meant so much to them growing up and they wanted to help when they heard wheelchair users couldn't always go. They committed to donate £1,000 for each of the next three seasons. Another local businessman, Richard Watkin from the Fat Boar restaurant, matched their donation. Seven matches a season became ten.

My initial plan for the second season had been to sell Wrexham cushions to keep seats warm on matchdays. I even made a prototype, asking Macron to print the club crest on a red seat cover from a garden centre. That one didn't even get off the ground because the club were worried that fans might throw them onto the pitch. I gave the one and only Kerry's red seat cover to my dad, who took it with him to games.

In 2021, Expedia became Wrexham's back-of-shirt sponsor. In 2023, however, they offered to sponsor the accessible away travel for the whole season, after which the fund merged into the away coach travel budget within the club. The accessible away travel takes care of itself now; it's just a service that runs alongside Pat's Coaches. Newer fans probably assume the service has always been there.

Nonetheless, I treasure the memory of my time selling blankets because people got behind what I was doing and were so grateful for the change we made. It was when I first became a voice for people with disabilities. The blankets' popularity raised my profile at the club and meant that anyone who didn't know how to find something or who had questions knew what to do: they could come to Kerry. With or without their red blankets.

# CHAPTER NINE

# THE QUIET ZONE

In October 2013, five years before the DLO role was established, Wrexham hosted Wales's first autism-friendly football match.

Autism, also known as autism spectrum disorder (ASD), is a condition that affects how people understand and interact with the world. It can make communication, socialising and everyday activities different for each person. Some may struggle with speaking or understanding emotions, whereas others might focus intensely on specific interests or prefer routines. It's called a spectrum because it varies a lot – everyone with autism is unique.

The autism-friendly match was against Woking, organised by Wrexham's Disabled Supporters Association. The DSA had been founded that same year as an independent committee of fans who wanted to help other people with disabilities become a part of Wrexham and raise funds for things to improve the club.

To host the game, the club, the DSA and the Wrexham Supporters Trust worked with a local charity called Autism Wishes, which makes dreams come true for autistic children and adults. It was one of the WST's four nominated charities that year. One boy whose special interest was buses got to ride on Pat's Coaches and ask questions. DSA chairman Steve Gilbert can be seen on YouTube videos discussing the positive impact of that day.

By all accounts, the DSA received lots of good feedback about the match. They let fans enter through gates instead of turnstiles, sat them in a quieter area away from the louder fans and allowed them to leave the ground and come back in if they needed to. Those fans had been invited to the ground a few days earlier to familiarise themselves with the layout and pointed in the direction of a staff member who would be their port of call throughout the game. As my role as DLO has become more established, the DSA's responsibilities have varied, but they still play a crucial part in organising all the blue badge parking in Wrexham University on a matchday and running and paying for the audio descriptive commentary service.

During those early months working with Colin, I was very aware of the success of the previous autism-friendly fixture at the club. *This is great*, I thought, *but hang on – we need to do more. Why just one day? What had they put in place that was so special that it could only be done for one fixture? Surely, we could do this for every game of the season.* I made this an early priority, firstly because it was something that the club had done before and secondly because it had been received so positively.

I reached out to the National Autistic Society (NAS) to arrange a meeting with Kerry Roberts, the Wrexham branch chair. Kerry's own daughter is autistic and nonverbal, and, like me, Kerry was a volunteer, doing her role for the love of making a difference for other families.

And at that stage, I didn't know anyone with autism. Kerry herself said that her early understanding of autism had been limited. After her own daughter was diagnosed, her perception of autism was bound up in her daughter's specific experience. Through her charity work, she came to realise how much the meaning of autism can vary, and that what would help one person may not help others.

For my first meeting with Kerry, I came armed with pages of notes on things we would be able to put in place very easily to improve the matchday experience.

I had started my research with lots of questions: how could we get people to the stands without taking them through the packed concourse? What can we provide once they're there? I tried to put myself in their shoes – what would they have difficulties with? I knew from my own experience that turnstiles can be very claustrophobic places, so could we open up the double doors to the Hays Travel stand to make an autism-friendly entrance and signpost them away from the noisy food queues? Could we give them space away from being in and among the caricatures of the beer-swilling, screaming football fans shouting at the referee and players, where they might find it difficult to distinguish that more abstract sense of anger from real anger and think they were in danger?

From there, I started working out answers. I plotted out what we now call our Quiet Route, which goes down the concrete walkway and along the full length of the front row. We could mark it out with the NAS signage so that people would know the route to follow. That could take them to our Quiet Zone: seats reserved only for people who need them. We could space out the seats so that each family had space around them. I thought the Quiet Zone could work well at the end of the Hays Travel stand because it's separated from the next section of seating by the stairwell, making it a safer, more easily controlled and moderated environment.

We would start off very small, with two or three families attending an area capable of seating 165 people. There, they'd be greeted with our familiar face stewards – the same people every matchday, to build that sense of comfort, routine and familiarity – who could offer out ear defenders, weighted blankets and fidget toys.

There was an accessible toilet in that area anyway, and I knew I'd be able to ringfence that for the Quiet Zone. I could get permission from the safety officer at the club for those fans to stay in their seats until the rest of the stand had emptied so that they didn't have to leave with the crowds.

Sensory rooms were a relatively new concept even at the highest division of football in 2018. Sunderland AFC had opened the very first four years earlier, but they only really spread more widely from 2017 onwards. I was very aware that Premier League clubs were beginning to install these much-needed additions in their hospitality areas, and I believed that Wrexham should have one too, accessible to all families in need of the Quiet Zone.

'And we'd build the sensory room around the back, underneath the stand,' I said to Kerry, combing through the rest of my notes. 'We've got a room there we can adapt. But – and this is a big but – you can't see it from the pitch. It's not massive. It's certainly not a fancy box like a lot of the Premier League clubs have. But it's the best we've got and the best we can do. I'm a volunteer; I'm not a professional.

'If we do those things,' I concluded, 'would they go towards advertising that we were autism-friendly?'

'If you can do those things,' she smiled, 'you're pretty much there.'

She said that she would work with me as I put my plans in place, after which I'd be able to apply to the NAS to get our official Autism Friendly Award. Every step of the way, she would back me. She promised to come to fixtures, meet families and spread the word at her branch meetings. There would be paperwork to fill out detailing all we'd put in place. I can say confidently that without her early endorsement, the Quiet Zone wouldn't have been so easy to build, because I wouldn't have had the confidence to know that I was doing the right things.

But that was all a long way off. First, I had to talk to the board.

'Here's what I'm proposing,' I said, talking them through what I'd discussed with Kerry. 'If I can have the first section of the Hays Travel stand as my Quiet Zone area, we'll be well on the way to fitting their criteria. No one is using that space. If I can take it over, we can bring in extra revenue from people that just wouldn't come without what I'm proposing we put in place. Otherwise, that section will just sit empty. We can open up a brand new revenue stream with all these new families that will want to be part of this.'

It was an instant yes. We had so few fans in those days that there was no shortage of space, and the existing eight season ticket holders in that section of the Hays Travel stand were incorporated into our Quiet Zone. (They weren't asked to move their seats until 2024, when there was increased demand for the service.)

I'd have to find the money, but I was confident I could do it. There were lots of avenues: quiz nights, donations and banging the drum on social media and in the local press. We now receive contributions from people who leave the club money in their will. In some cases, they've specified that they wanted the money to go to the Quiet Zone.

The sensory room started life as a disused kiosk, used as an unofficial storage room, at the far end of the stand. Location-wise, it was perfect: right next to the accessible toilet and in an area of the stand that fans don't use until they're exiting at the end of the game, so it was quiet.

It was two years before we were able to board up the shutters to make it into a proper room in its own right, but that wasn't our biggest problem. The room didn't even have a ceiling. It stretched instead up to the top of the stand, and you could see the concrete zig-zag of rows of seats. It smacked of neglect: it was freezing, covered in cobwebs and the steel girder holding up the stand was flaking red paint.

Kings and I cleared the room. He whitewashed the walls and sandpapered the girder, repainting it bright red. We relied heavily on volunteers and charitable local businesses.

I contacted the outside contractor, Mike of White and Williams, who takes on lots of jobs for the club.

'Can you give me a price?' I asked, as he surveyed the room.

He shook his head. 'We'll sort this for free.'

Mike erected a false ceiling, boarded up the kiosk serving hatch and fitted a new work surface and a Radar key. Matt from Barlow's upgraded the electrics and installed spotlights, a TV and a heater.

What we hadn't realised is that when there was heavy rain, it drained to both ends of Hays Travel stand. Our end of the stadium flooded pretty regularly. Our new carpet had been down a matter of weeks before the whole thing was underwater. We tried to dry it out, but the stench told us we were chasing a lost cause. We went back to Castle Mews Carpets and they put in a bright red safety floor that could just be mopped.

All these companies bought into what we were doing and recognised that I needed help. The work of volunteers meant that we did everything for about £300. One contractor wanted to help because his son is autistic and we had a fruitful conversation about what we needed for the area. 'This is important to me,' he said. 'It's important that all these people feel welcome and can access the club.'

We've upgraded the room several times since then, but to begin with, a narrow kitchen worktop ran in an L-shape around the room.

That was where we put our books and fidget spinners. I put a lot of research into the kind of books to stock: braille books, books about autism, Makaton books. We started with the basics: red blankets, ear defenders, a braille puzzle cube, a couple of red chairs, fluffy red cushions.

As time's gone on, we've been able to add things. Our waitress service was made available once the stands got busier – if someone needed the Quiet Zone, there was a good chance they'd struggle to queue on a bustling, tight concourse for refreshments. Now, we have over £2,000 worth of equipment, including an infinity mirror, teddies and weighted blankets. We leave a weighted blanket on the seat of one little boy before he arrives because the first thing he does is wrap himself up. Not everyone needs those supports, but that's the point: everyone is different. Some fans don't rely on them, but others couldn't cope without.

I saw a Kopy Kat interactive wall panel when visiting a wellbeing hub in Wrexham city centre and reached out to the finance department to buy it with the last of the money that people had donated specifically to help me with my role. When idle, the machine plays music, and one of the songs on its playlist is the theme tune to *It's Always Sunny in Philadelphia*. I'm convinced whoever programmed that machine did it as a joke especially for us; Kings thinks it's just a coincidence. In July 2021, I paid an artist, Ellie Humphreys, to paint a mural of the Hays Travel stand along with sunflowers, the symbol for hidden disabilities. In August 2023, another artist, Michelle Edwards, added some inspirational quotes to finally complete the room.

That all came later. Our initial sensory room was basic, but we were never opening the Quiet Zone without it.

I half apologised before opening the door to the assessor Sarah

Morgan, from the Wales branch of the NAS, when she came in 2018. 'We've done our best,' I started, 'but I know the hub isn't ideal. It's a very small room.' I watched with bated breath as she ran her eyes over what we'd spent the last few months making.

'This is absolutely amazing,' she said. 'This is just what is needed. There are Premier League clubs who spent £30,000–£40,000 on sensory rooms, hiring specialist companies to do up their boxes. Families can watch the game from the boxes, but they have to prebook and watch the match from there. You've done the right thing. The whole point of families coming to the stadium is to watch a match in the stands, and you've given them this as an option if they're struggling. They can take ten minutes or half an hour.' She paused and looked at me with a firm smile. 'Stop apologising. This is just as good as all those other clubs.'

We got our NAS Autism Friendly Award on 27 November 2018, a milestone celebrated on a Saturday fixture day. The club were not keen on a wheelchair user tearing up the pitch at half time for the presentation, so it was decided that, as this was an event all about the Quiet Zone, the presentation should take place in front of that area. At half time, the commentary team interviewed us all. We were the first club to achieve autism-friendly status in Wales and the first autism-friendly business in Wrexham.

We attracted families I'd never met before thanks to the NAS spreading the word. We launched with quiet walkabout sessions so that anybody who wanted to see our facilities could come and meet me while the stadium was closed. I would show them the Quiet Zone, the toilets and the sensory hub, and answer any questions.

At our first quiet walkabout, I met fans who had come to the initial autism-friendly game back in 2013. The very first child I welcomed underlined just how important it was that we get this right.

He had never been to a football match before, but arrived with his parents, and as I greeted him outside the ground, music boomed from the huge speakers in the beer garden at The Turf pub. He visibly shrank, his head curling into his chest, pulled his hood up and burst into tears. He settled again once we moved him away. He's a teenager now and still comes to our Quiet Zone, where he has a season ticket.

The stories I heard on these walkabouts were varied, but many told me that they couldn't have come to Wrexham for the first time with 3,500 people in the stands. Visiting while the stadium was empty gave them the confidence to return. I promised them that before every fixture, I would be waiting outside the same double doors through which they'd entered. If, for whatever reason, they ran into trouble, I'd be there.

Some people won't come to a game if I'm not there. I'm part of their routine: they see me, chat to me and then their matchday process gets underway. I'm their familiar face.

We learned other things as time went on. We turned down the volume on the PA system in that area. Parents requested an analogue clock for the Quiet Zone: routine is important for autistic people and those parents said that it would be helpful to talk their children through what would happen and when.

In 2023, I paid out of the budget for an official Makaton trainer. Makaton uses symbols (pictures) and signs (hand gestures) alongside speech to help those who struggle to communicate. Lots of the children who come to the Quiet Zone are nonverbal or have delayed speech. Being able to welcome people using Makaton, even if we only have short conversations, makes them feel safer. That's always been at the heart of what we do in the Quiet Zone, and the children's confidence increases as they don't have to endure the frustration of being unable to explain how they feel or what they need. Awareness of Makaton is constantly increasing and even children with no speech issues find they benefit from learning it. My granddaughter, Hali, will be taught how to sign at nursery.

I knew someone working in the children's ward of the local hospital who was trained in Makaton and they gave me the details of the woman who had coached her. The instructor, Amanda, kindly offered to run a training session via Zoom, so I contacted everyone at the club to see who would be interested in taking part in the session. Lots signed up: people from the media team, the foundation, the club shop, the man who played the club mascot Wrex the Dragon, stewards and, of course, my staff from the Quiet Zone. Ben Tozer, the Wrexham centre half, also joined the call. Whenever I saw him after that, he'd sign to me.

The initial training took just an hour, but moving through the other levels involved classroom work over several weeks. Amanda eventually helped us work through what were then known as Levels 2, 3 and 4 to earn, by the summer of 2023, our Makaton gold standard certification (they don't rank their accreditation in that way any more).

One father of twins had only ever been able to take one of his sons to matches before. At his first match in the Quiet Zone, he was in floods of tears. At full time, he approached me and wiped his eyes. 'You don't realise what this meant to me,' he said. 'You don't know what it means to be with both of my boys at the football.'

One dad reached out to me not long after his son had received an autism diagnosis. As a family, they were struggling to deal with it. 'It's like he doesn't know how to speak to me,' he said to me one day. After Wrexham's win in the final game of the 2022/23 season, he had tears in his eyes for a different reason. 'You've given me my son back,' he told me. 'What you've built here is absolutely incredible. We're absolutely loving doing this together. And I don't think you realise how powerful this is.' It was an incredibly emotional reminder of the importance of our Quiet Zone.

I hear those kinds of comments a lot. I don't say that to be flippant or conceited, but to show just how vital this kind of service is. So many people say that without our Quiet Zone, they could never attend Wrexham matches. If football clubs aren't willing to listen to the needs of neurodiverse fans and their families, the game will remain closed off to millions of people.

• • •

'Do you do any football sessions?'

'Do you do any coaching for them?'

I was fielding an increasing number of calls and emails like this, and they were right: we should be running football sessions for the families attending our Quiet Zone and autistic children within our community.

I reached out to what was, at that time, Wrexham AFC Community Trust: 'You know when you run your half term soccer schools? Can we do an autism-friendly football session?'

As ever, I'd sat down earlier with a blank piece of paper and a question: we have all these kids who can't come to our existing soccer schools and it's not fair that they're missing out, so what can we provide to cater to them?

The existing soccer schools ran for four hours each day, Monday to Friday, in the half term. They were outside, but that would be a barrier for us because the weather could be changeable and throw off some kids. We had to make sure that the setting was the same every time: the same coaches, the same weather and the same temperature. We hired the sports hall in Wrexham University for a one-hour session on a Monday each half term, initially for all ages before splitting into primary and secondary school groups once the soccer schools took off.

I advertised the sessions as child-centric. We had to have a structure, because twenty kids running riot wouldn't be good for anybody, but it would be a loose one. Taking precedent would be the capabilities of the children and their needs. One child, aged about three, came in with his dad, who was holding him in his arms like a baby.

'I've brought him, but he won't even join in,' said the dad.

'That's absolutely fine,' I assured him. 'Let him watch. Do whatever he wants to do.'

Within fifteen minutes, he took a ball and played in a corner on his own for the whole session. 'That's the point,' I said to his dad. 'It's about doing exactly what they want in the way that works for them.'

Many families approached me and asked us to expand our soccer schools offering – one hour once a week just wasn't enough.

'We need to start seeing if we could hold these more regularly,' Wrexham striker Paul Mullin said to me one day. 'Leave it with me and I'll see what I can do.' His son, Albi, is autistic, and I know that Paul really values what we've done for families with autistic children. When we had reporters in to discuss our autism-friendly soccer school provision, Paul was front and centre.

That said, the Quiet Zone serves so much more than autistic fans and their families. Mike, for instance, first came to a quiet walk-about session with a nurse from Wrexham Maelor Hospital. He was an outpatient, but he was having an awful lot of support and counselling. His nurse did all of the talking with me about dates and meeting points. I met this man who stood with his head down and never spoke. He was a shell of a person.

'It's going to be hard, isn't it, Mike?' she said to him. 'Coming on your own will be tough. Could he bring somebody with him? I think it would be so good for you, Mike, to have this in your life.' She explained that he didn't go anywhere or have any hobbies.

Mike is now one of my biggest success stories. He comes bubbly to the door and never misses a match but has said he would find it stressful without me being at Gate 12 to welcome him. I advised him to fill out the paperwork for PIP so that he could bring a companion free of charge. He absolutely loves it and is a completely different person to the one I first met.

For the fourth series of *Welcome to Wrexham*, the crew worked with a lady who was once so ill with anxiety that she walked into the club shop and tried to return her season ticket with more than half the matches left to play. 'I just can't deal with coming anymore,' Ann said. 'Give my season ticket to someone else.' The staff in the club shop passed her number to me and I showed her around our facilities. She's made so many friends now with the people in our Quiet Zone, and her story demonstrates that what we offer is fulfilling for all kinds of people for lots of different reasons. I have another woman who is very reclusive and had never been to a football match before, but travels quite a distance, alone, and enjoys coming to Wrexham because she knows she'll be safe and secure.

The Quiet Zone isn't a cure-all. Sometimes people just freeze and can't come to the ground even with everything we have in place. When that happens, I'll call their families and check in after a few days. Some of the people we welcome don't have friends or hobbies. They can't go to school or work. Some of them don't go anywhere during the week. Their families, and Wrexham, become their world.

I have countless other families for whom football is something they do together and it becomes a lifeline for them. Every so often, people feel able to leave our stand and sit elsewhere. Some are fine, but others return. We'll always be there for them, and we do our best to accommodate everyone, whatever their needs.

The Quiet Zone has become a community in its own right, one in which everybody is there for each other and is respectful of each other's needs. The stewards I work with are a really significant part of that. One of them is Nicky, who, during the week, works for a charity called Home-Start Wrexham, which empowers families in need with parenting skills to ensure positive outcomes for years to come. We're incredibly lucky to have her and, away from the club, Kings and I are close with her and her husband Jason, who is also a steward. Nicky has become another one of my best friends, and I really value our special connection.

Our other long-serving Quiet Zone steward is Amy, who is very experienced at her job and a huge help with our waitress service. She told me that working in our Quiet Zone has made her a better, more understanding parent. That our work has had such an impact is the biggest compliment, I feel.

Chiefly, I look for empathy within my stewards. Anyone who works in the Quiet Zone needs to know how to talk to the families, how to relate to them, what they can say and what they can't. Some people, for example, instinctively ignore nonverbal or selectively mute children, but we talk to them and include them in the conversation, even if we're just answering our own questions. Parents appreciate that – but why wouldn't I involve their kids? They just need to do things in their own time and at their own pace. They don't deserve to be ignored.

Where all the other stewards are paid to watch the crowds, mine are paid to sit down, have a natter with the families and make them feel welcome. You get a lot of TLC in my area.

Having a Quiet Zone within a football stadium is certainly unique. Lots of people recognise this. In 2022, TV presenter Jeff Brazier visited the Racecourse to cover a match for TV and met me on his way out of the ground. 'The Racecourse was heaving again today!' he later tweeted. 'Congratulations Kerry Evans, @Wrexham_AFC disability liaison officer, leading the club's inclusivity efforts. It was amazing to see the autism-friendly section being enjoyed by so many.'

I'm incredibly proud of our Quiet Zone and all it represents to enable fans who otherwise couldn't sit among the crowds to watch live sport at Wrexham. They feel safe and secure while enjoying the fixtures.

One of the boys I work with, Theo, picked me as the focus for his school International Women's Day project. 'I chose Kerry as my inspirational woman to celebrate International Women's Day because she has such a positive impact on my life,' he wrote.

She works incredibly hard to ensure all the disabled football supporters have what they need in place to feel welcome and enjoy watching and playing football. Kerry champions all disabilities and all fans, home and away, but her work with autism and other hidden disabilities has changed my life. Some of my happiest memories are because of her and that is why I think she deserves to be celebrated today.

I wanted to end this chapter with a comment from one of the families who use the Quiet Zone, so that they can explain in their own words what it means to them.

Before we started to attend the Quiet Zone, we had no support. My son struggled to leave the house, stopped being able to attend school and was unable to continue playing football – which was his biggest passion. We had no support, and life was very lonely for the both of us. We struggled with being misunderstood and not having anywhere 'safe' and welcoming. A place where we both felt we were understood and not judged was so hard to find.

The moment we came to the Quiet Zone, we knew we had found something special. Kerry, all the staff and other users made us feel so welcome. All my son's needs are catered for, and I've found so much support for myself from other parents who have had the same experiences as us. To see my son feel so comfortable out of the house, and to see him smile, laugh and cheer, has been the most amazing experience. When times have been hard, there is always someone to talk to and lean on for support. Kerry has been an amazing support for me and is always trying to help in any way she can.

Life for neurodivergent children and their parents can be so tough, with tears, stress and constantly having to fight for your child. But when you come to the football, you can just switch off and be part of something so amazing. We would be lost without the Quiet Zone. Thank you for creating something truly special.

– Helen

# CHAPTER TEN

# THE TAKEOVER

I didn't enter the Racecourse for a whole year.

Covid ripped across the world, and my existing conditions and weakened immune system meant that I was at high risk of serious illness if I caught the virus. Kings and I were advised to shield, and we followed all the rules to the letter. One doctor had even told me that if I ever went into intensive care – which was almost a certainty if I tested positive – medical staff would prioritise other patients because my litany of health problems meant that I would be more difficult to save. It was a terrifying thing to hear.

Delivery drivers knew that I was vulnerable so left our groceries on the doorstep. We would wipe everything down at the front door, disinfecting it before we dared to take it into the kitchen. By the time Dad's seventieth birthday came around, restrictions had been tightened to the point that the police stopped anyone crossing country lines. Mum, Dad, Kings and I met on the border, right under the sign for Wrexham, to exchange presents. Even then I kept my distance. Nan sent a video for my birthday: 'Hi, Kerry – this is your nan,' it began, as if I didn't know. Mum filmed it from the outside of Nan's house, through the open window. You could see my mum's reflection in the glass.

Casey was in her second year of training for her nursing degree and working at Wrexham Maelor Hospital. The staff there told her in no uncertain terms that she would not be able to complete her placement if she was to continue living with me – it would just be too risky. Casey moved out and into a house with her boyfriend Rhys. I felt guilty about that, even though she understood why she had to go. We only spoke on video calls.

My brother Ian, meanwhile, was among the millions of people in the arts industry who found himself looking for other work. He helped elderly people around Bexhill-on-Sea with shopping and collecting medications just to feel like he was doing his bit.

I coped because, ultimately, I felt safe in the house out of harm's way. Covid absolutely petrified me. In the past, doctors had told me that I have 'practically no immune system to speak of', and any sort of cold or cough Kings or Casey brought in always knocked me out for weeks on end. What if anything were to get in the house now?

Staying indoors stripped away all the worries and anxieties about being exposed to the virus and a part of me enjoyed being off-grid. I'm lucky in that I enjoy my own company, and I still had Kings. In so many ways, we were far more fortunate than the millions of families who suffered so much during that time. Even after the vaccination rollout, it was difficult to start going out again. This was life or death for me, as it was for so many others, and I was so frightened to take any risks.

The football club, meanwhile, had issues of its own. The 2019/20 season had ended prematurely because of the pandemic, and this was probably the only thing that saved Wrexham from relegation to the sixth tier. This would not just have been a reputational blow: the players would have been made part-time, in need of other jobs to supplement their club wages. Instead, the National League ranking

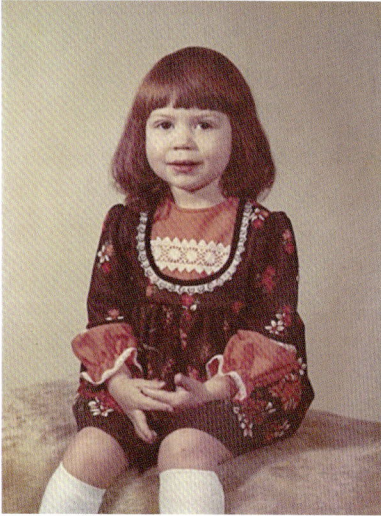

Posing for the camera in my new Christmas dress, aged three. Although I was born with cerebral palsy, my parents didn't find out until I was about a year old. There were only a couple of signs that something was wrong: I walked on the ball of my right foot and when I concentrated, I clenched my fist.

My mum, Sue, and my dad, Phil, who have always been my strongest supporters. I couldn't have wished for better parents. They had very little professional help after they discovered that I had cerebral palsy, but they were always caring and encouraging. Even when I found activities tricky due to my condition, they pushed me to not give up; I took classes at my mum's dance school until I was eight and when they became too difficult, my parents bought me my first pony, Bianco, and my dad helped me care for her.

My wonderful grandparents on my mum's side, Vera and Idris Roberts, were both really important figures in my life growing up. After Granddad passed, Nan and I remained very close and spoke nearly every day.

The Jones siblings together. Me at sixteen, with Ian (*left*), aged eleven, and Matt (*right*), aged four. Ian and I were very close growing up. Because I moved out when Matt was young, our relationship grew stronger as we both got older.

The Jones siblings all grown up and on a cruise to celebrate my parents' fiftieth wedding anniversary in 2023. Ian (*right*) is an actor and Matt (*left*), following in Dad's footsteps, has a high-powered career and is head of his department.

My family! Back row (from *left* to *right*): Kings, Lizzii, Ian, Uncle Glyn, Auntie Carol, Dad, Mum, Matt, Holly, Callum, Paul, Josie, Georgine and Mark. Front row (from *left* to *right*): Ellis, Georgie, me and Nan.

Out with Joanne, my best friend since I was six, for my hen party in 2002. She had always said that Kings, my soon-to-be husband, was the person for me and she was absolutely right.

A friendship that has lasted a lifetime. Joanne has stayed with me through thick and thin. She was one of the few people who didn't treat me any differently after my cerebral bleed.

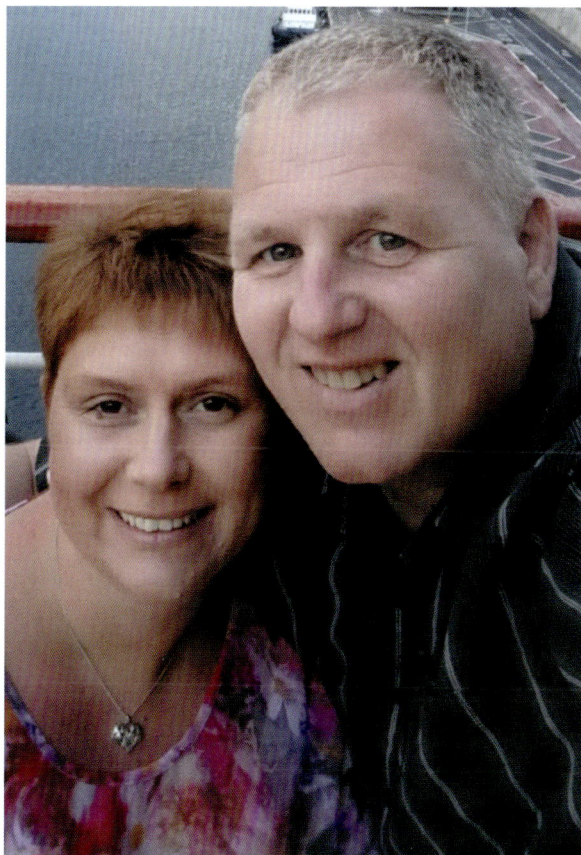

With my amazing husband, Kings, on a cruise in 2017. We met through a mutual friend when I was working at a car garage. He was my best friend for years and then he became my everything. He's always been my inspiration and my rock.

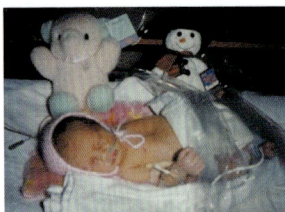

ABOVE My daughter Casey, born prematurely on Christmas Eve 1997. I hadn't realised that I was pregnant until shortly before she was delivered via emergency Caesarean section.

RIGHT Four generations of my family, including a very tiny Casey shortly after she was released from the hospital. Kings, Casey and I could finally begin our wonderful new life together.

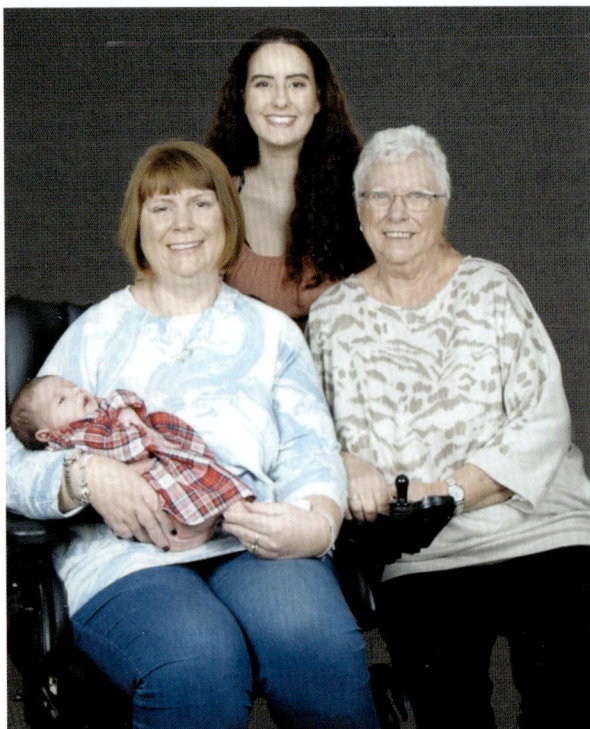

RIGHT The next four generations, celebrating the birth of my granddaughter Hali in 2023. I was in the room to support Casey as Hali was born and it was the greatest honour of my lifetime.

Me and Kings with Casey on our wedding day in 2002. Casey was one of my bridesmaids, along with Lowri, Kings's niece, and Joanne was my maid of honour.

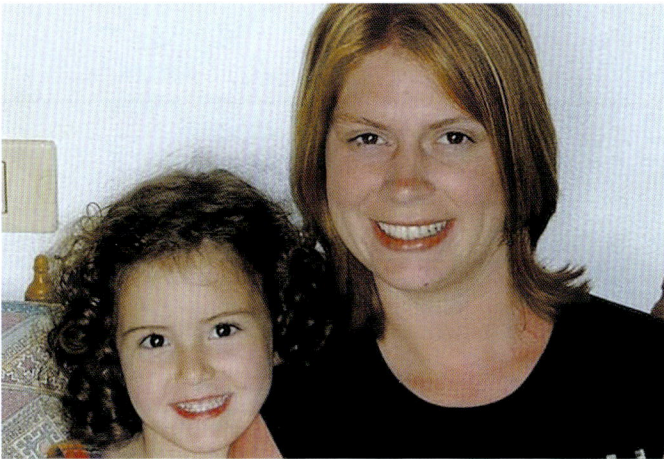

Me and Casey, aged five, on holiday in Lanzarote in 2003. Casey was just like my brother Ian was at school – bright, popular and great at sports!

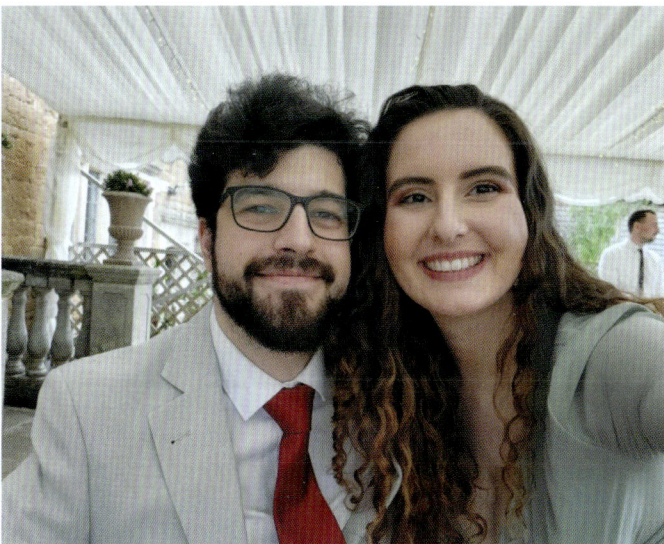

Casey with her fiancé, Rhys. Casey is a qualified neonatal nurse and is training to become a health visitor.

Me holding Hali for the first time. I'm her *nain* (nana) and Kings is her *taid* (granddad), and we have the most beautiful bond.

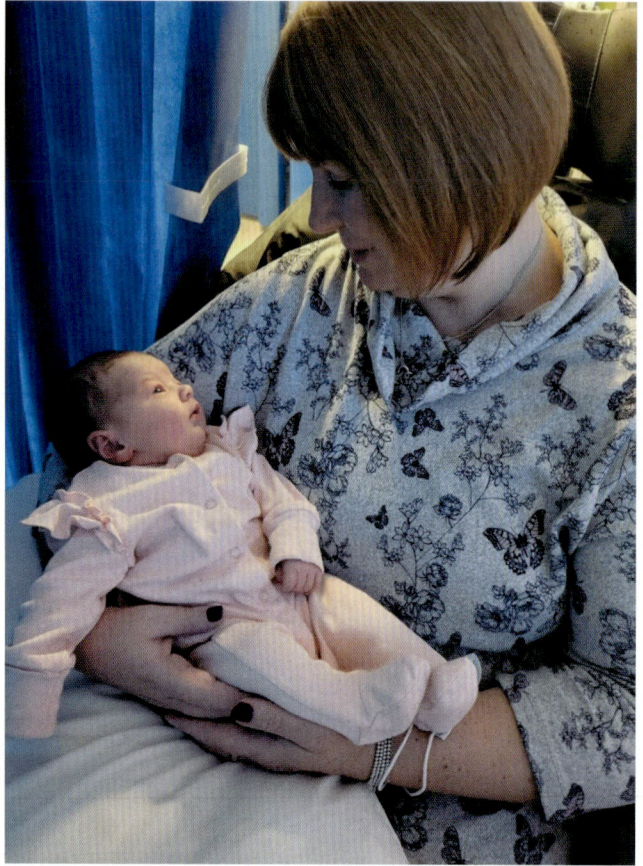

Baby Hali – she'll always be a Wrexham fan! © Leah Dolimore

One of my favourite pictures with Dad at the LDV Vans Trophy (the Vertu Trophy as of 2024) final at the Millennium (now Principality) Stadium, Cardiff, in 2005, which Wrexham won 2–0 against Southend United. Shortly afterwards, I had a life-altering cerebral bleed.

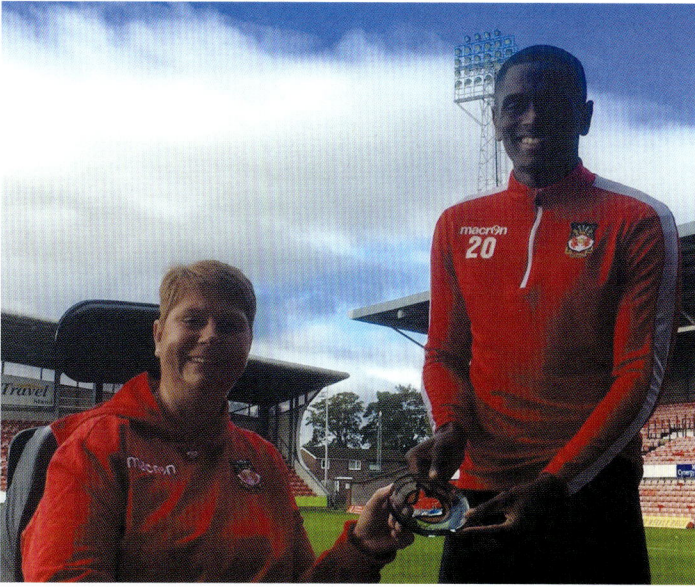

Former Wrexham midfielder Akil Wright presenting me with the National League Volunteer of the Month award in September 2018 in recognition of my work at Wrexham AFC as a volunteer – in particular, the funding of the Quiet Zone through selling 'Kerry's red blankets', collecting donations and organising sponsors.

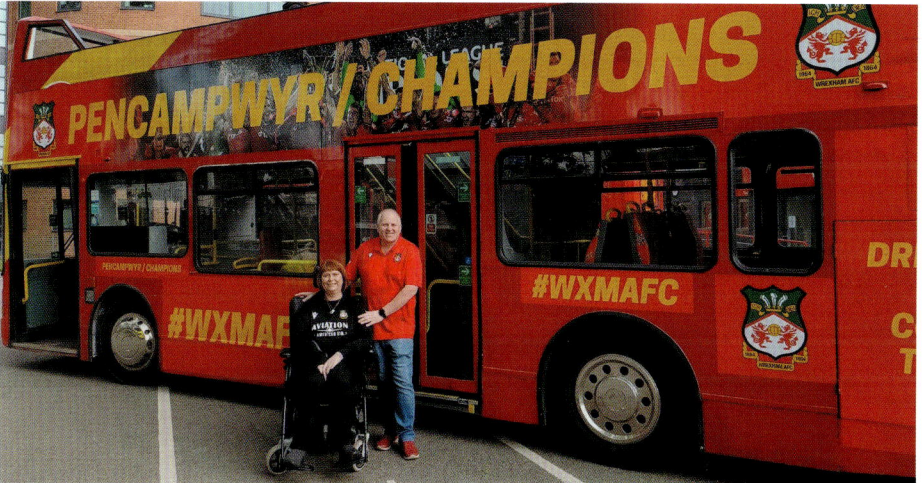

ABOVE Over 40,000 people turned up for Wrexham's open-top bus parade, which marked the club's promotion out of the National League in April 2023. I rode on one of the buses, which is a hugely special memory.

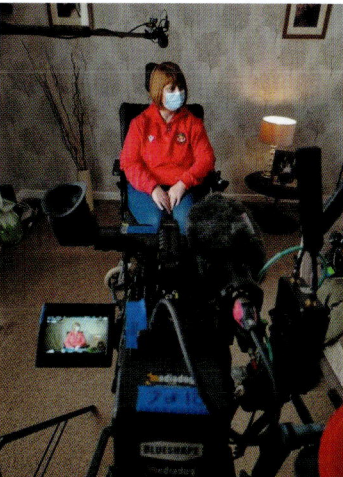

LEFT Behind the scenes of filming for *Welcome to Wrexham* in our front room in May 2022. I was nervous about how the show would represent me, but the crew and the production team did a fantastic job.

Meeting King Charles and Queen Camilla, with Rob McElhenney and Ryan Reynolds looking on, during their royal visit to confer Wrexham's new city status in December 2022. It was a huge honour to introduce Wrexham's powerchair football team and discuss my work with them.

My most touching interaction with Ryan took place on the weekend of his and Rob's first visit to Wrexham in October 2021. Ryan asked me to come on board as a full-time member of staff and this photo captures the moment he said: 'Kerry, if my girls grow up to be anything like you, I'll be the proudest dad alive.' © Robert Stead was decided on points per game, and Wrexham stayed in because they had amassed 0.08 points per game more than Eastleigh FC. That twentieth-placed finish was Wrexham's lowest in their entire 156 years of football.

The Wrexham Supporters Trust furloughed the players on 80 per cent pay, with no idea when matches would resume. At one point, the players were doing their strength and conditioning programmes in their gardens, and some took on other work at supermarkets or as delivery drivers to help provide for their families. Our captain, Shaun Pearson, was a driver for the Fat Boar and delivered my birthday meal to the house, with a free birthday cake sent by Rich Watkin, the restaurant's co-owner.

Like many people during this period, I worked from home every day; I wasn't needed at the ground if we didn't have any fixtures. Spencer Harris was the one person at Wrexham who would always call to check how I was, either first thing in the morning or last thing at night. Spencer's preference for video calls meant that I would squirm at the thought of him seeing me in my pyjamas, but those chats were a lifeline to the club when so many felt isolated and cut adrift. I will be forever grateful for his support.

My main memory of Spencer's calls are his worries and his realism: that the longer all this went on, the harder and harder it would be to keep Wrexham alive. To put it bluntly, the worst-case scenario was that the club would cease to exist.

All I could do was hope and pray that we would get through. What could I do to help? People had already, years ago, emptied their pockets and handed over their house deeds to save the club. How much would they have left to give? This time, they were struggling, too. It all felt out of our control.

When football resumed the following season, it was without fans in the stands. Kings and I paid each week to follow matches via the club's streaming service, which the WST ran using a special camera that tracked the movement of the ball so that they didn't need a camera operator on site. Those stream passes were the only form of revenue for the club during that time, but watching, from home, matches taking place in a silent, deserted stadium quickly made many fans feel even more detached and disconnected from the club. There was no chance of me going to the ground to peek through the gates like some fans did. We didn't know, back then, who else had been watching those streams.

This is the Wrexham that Ryan and Rob stepped into.

•   •   •

I, of course, would find out their names earlier on in the process than most Wrexham fans, who, to begin with, knew only that the club had caught the attention of two high-net-worth individuals – or, in the words of the *Wrexham Leader*: 'well-known individuals of financial means'.

Before we could learn any more, Wrexham Supporters Trust members had to vote on whether we should move forward and entertain further talks with the pair. Over a Zoom call, we were told that their plan was to buy Wrexham for a nominal charge of £1 and invest a minimum of £2 million.

Really, there wasn't any decision to make. The pandemic meant that the club was already struggling and there was no end to that in sight, which meant no easy route back to financial health for a fan-owned club. What was the choice? Struggle and go down to National League North in the sixth tier – or see where these conversations went.

In a vote, 1,223 of Wrexham Supporters Trust members voted to open talks. The next day, they learned the names: Ryan Reynolds and Rob McElhenney.

'Ryan Reynolds!' screamed Casey as we filled her in the next day. She and Kings had watched quite a lot of Ryan's films, including *Deadpool*. I hadn't. I only ever really watch romcoms.

'Are you serious?!' Casey gasped, when I told her this. 'Do you not—' She opened his Wikipedia page and began racing through his credits.

'*Deadpool*?'

'No.'

'*Detective Pikachu*?'

'No.'

'*The Proposal*?'

'No.'

'This is *wasted* on you!'

It didn't really matter that I hadn't seen him act, because his name preceded him. Who hadn't heard of him? It was obvious what his money and star power could mean for Wrexham.

What I don't think we appreciated was the breadth of his business portfolio, which included his production company Maximum Effort and stakes in Aviation American Gin and Mint Mobile. Lots of his ventures were US-based so we hadn't heard of them, but anyone who read between the lines might have concluded that Wrexham was about to become a story of its own and Ryan Reynolds had the means to document it all. Indeed, within a few days rumours circulated that Ryan and Rob were suggesting filming a documentary on the club as part of their proposed takeover.

Once the feeling of disbelief had subsided, I think the majority of Wrexham fans were nervous and wary. Their chief concern was

Ryan and Rob's motive: were they doing this for the right reasons or was this just a PR stunt? What was in it for them? Where would we all be once they'd finished filming this documentary – whatever that entailed? Would the club become a media circus or, worse, a laughing stock? And what would happen to the ground, the team and the club once they lost interest?

Yes, it sounded like a fairy tale. But… well… why? Why Wrexham?

This feeling was especially intense because Wrexham supporters had had their fingers burnt by unscrupulous owners in the past. It made them understandably suspicious. That would have been the case even if a local businessman expressed interest, but international stars from LA and Vancouver added another layer of confusion to it all. Even with the documentary added into the equation, it still made little sense.

Working in Ryan and Rob's favour was the fact that the club had just endured such a difficult season on the field. An increasing number of fans had begun to express cynicism about the Wrexham Supporters Trust and were keen to go in a new direction. Frustration grew because year after year fans watched teams with more money buy up the best players and leapfrog us to promotion. There was a ray of hope in May 2018 when the former Wales international Sam Ricketts took over as Wrexham manager on a three-year contract and promotion felt like a possibility… until Ricketts left for Shrewsbury Town in December, with Wrexham fourth in the table – one place away from the National League play-offs. Ricketts was replaced by interim manager Graham Barrow, and we finished fifth overall.

That was the reality of Wrexham at the time. We were trying to do it our way, the best we knew how, but in a league that was notoriously tricky to get out of, our way was also the hard way. With each new season in the National League, it felt like the challenge was getting tougher.

Fans very much felt like Wrexham was *their* club – they could wander around the stadium, talk to players and goings on were never secret for long – so they were never shy in voicing their opinion when the going got tough. Directors were often under scrutiny at the WST. People didn't always agree with their decisions or know their motivations and felt entitled to say that. The pandemic heightened the appetite for change because no one knew what the club's finances would look like if things continued as they were.

But the counterpoint to any criticism of the Trust was that the club simply wouldn't exist without it. My view was that Wrexham being fan-owned was really special. Everybody felt that they were doing their bit towards keeping it going. Our team wasn't a big player on the global stage, but it was ours – a Wrexham club owned by Wrexham people. That came with a particular sense of belonging that was very precious, especially in an era where there is so much money (not all of it clean) floating around at the highest levels of football. People were anxious about losing all that was pure and humble about the club – that its integrity would be compromised.

'Ultimately, these two are not going to put their reputations on the line to then do something really bad,' Kings concluded one day. 'They're not just shady businessmen you've never heard of. One of them is an international movie star. Why would he do something that could end his career? Ryan Reynolds is not going to leave with his tail between his legs.'

In November, the day after I received the phone call from Rob, each member of the WST received an email inviting them to a Q&A session with Ryan and Rob via Zoom. First, the club needed to upgrade its Zoom subscription to one that could accommodate more than a thousand people. All our meetings had only ever taken place in the Centenary Club. Even without the pandemic, that venue wouldn't have been big enough to hold all the fans on the call. It made me chuckle to think that Rob's parting words to me were 'see you on the call' – as if he'd be able to see me at all with that many participants!

For the first hour, Ryan and Rob would outline their vision and take questions from the roughly 1,300 fans on the call. For the last half an hour, they would log off the call and fans would voice their views on what they'd just heard.

Interviewing Ryan and Rob would be James Harrison, a prison officer and volunteer for the media team whose experience commentating on matches and conducting post-match interviews with players and managers made him the best choice. He had also worked with the fundraising committee organising events, raffles and auctions with prizes like stadium tours and meet-and-greets with the players to find the budget for transfers and repairs. During the pandemic, he had been one of the members trying to make the finances add up.

James and the committee had spoken to Ryan and Rob via video call the day previously. Ryan was filming *Red Notice* with Dwayne Johnson, and at one point, the Rock appeared in the background of Ryan's call asking Ryan to come to set. James was also in the process of moving house and without internet, so had to host the whole thing from his stepdad's office in his mum's house.

Ryan and Rob had to convince the WST to give up the club – the same fans who had almost lost their club, first to previous owners and now the pandemic. There was pressure on them to convince us that they were in all this for the right reasons, that we could safely pass the club over to strangers who, by their own admission, didn't know much about football.

The Trust board contacted owners in advance to explain the stipulations put to Ryan and Rob. They were forbidden, for example, from moving from the Racecourse until the day it became apparent that the club needed a bigger stadium. The Trust also kept hold of the lease for the stadium, which was a key part of Ryan and Rob proving that they could be trusted.

After my phone call with Rob, I was even more certain of their promises and intentions. I expected that they would reassure the fans that they were genuine and serious, that their presence would only ever be positive.

All this time later, that phone call still feels like a dream. It was certainly a dream come true, that's for sure. Rob had told me that he and Ryan were nervous for the Q&A because they didn't know what to expect, how the fans would react or which way the vote would go. If Ryan or Rob were approaching a chairman or CEO of an ordinary company, they would have to convince a board of directors – but this would be far more public, with more voices offering questions and opinions. Some of those messages would be straightforward (some really did just message James to say 'hi' to Ryan and Rob during the call), but the rest would emphasise just how seriously the fans took the running of their club.

All members received an encrypted message with their unique link to log on to the call, ensuring that no one from outside the Trust could join. That Sunday night, we logged on to be greeted by the smiling faces of Rob and Ryan. Back in their homes, the cameras were already rolling. Should the takeover go through, this would have to feature.

'We want to take the opportunity to lay out for you our vision for what we believe is a bright future together,' Rob started. 'But we should start with that first very important question – and I'm sure it's one that everybody on this call is wondering – which is: why Wrexham?'

'We believe that your club is a sleeping giant,' Ryan explained. 'You have a wonderful and incredibly storied history, an incredible stadium which already draws thousands of supporters. I think the only thing that might be missing here is the resources to kick it to where it has always belonged. It has always belonged in league football. We have those resources and the ability to grow the exposure in a way I don't think Wrexham has had before. For a club with this potential, we really think the sky's the limit.'

I was filled with a peculiar on-the-brink feeling: a realisation that there was going to be life before this moment and life after it. I felt like I was watching a wave building, with all of us about to ride it. 'Watershed moment' doesn't do this justice. Ryan and Rob were about to pull us into a new world – possibly on a bigger scale than we could even comprehend. At the time, how could we imagine Wrexham, our tiny town, going global? I was hearing their words, but they weren't sinking in.

Rob said that he had spent hours researching the club, watching old footage and poring over photographs in which he saw the very kind of people he had grown up with in Philadelphia. His great-great-grandfather, he added, was a coal miner in northern England and Scotland. Rob was keen to emphasise his respect for the club's history and values: his approach for the call, he told us, had been to think about all the things he would want to hear if someone took over his beloved Philadelphia Eagles, Philadelphia Phillies or Philadelphia Flyers.

He and Ryan promised 'comprehensive financial support', to hire 'a proper CEO with vast experience running clubs at a very, very high level', to invest in a permanent training facility, to refurbish the Racecourse and, most importantly, that the club 'cannot be relocated, renamed or rebranded'.

'We are going to ensure, without a doubt, the continued presence of Dixie McNeil as the club's honorary president,' Rob continued. 'That's subject to his desire, but I can give you a little update on that. I did speak with Dixie this past week, and he's very excited and we're excited to have him. He'll be there for as long as he wants to be.'

Kings and I knew that would go down well with the fans. Dixie McNeil is a superstar in Wrexham, a former striker and manager who is not only widely regarded as one of the club's greatest ever players but also one of the nicest guys you could wish to meet. He still comes to all the Wrexham matches.

'We're going to, of course, expand the club staff to take advantage of the increased interest in Wrexham, both locally and internationally,' Rob went on. 'We want to recognise Wrexham's role as a leading force for the community in the town, and this is such a huge part of why we're doing this and what we want to try to accomplish. It's not just about the club, but it's about the club's role in the community. We're going to work with the club's disability liaison officer, Kerry Evans, who I've actually already spoken to this past week. She's very excited. We're very excited to work with her. We want to just continue to enhance Wrexham's reputation as being an inclusive and forward-thinking club, alongside some of the other local groups such as the Racecourse Community Foundation and, of course, food banks and local schools.'

I gasped as my phone buzzed at the side of me. It was Mum. 'They've just mentioned you!' she shrieked. 'They've just said your name!'

When I hung up, there were scores of messages from everyone else I knew: 'We've just heard your name!' they read, or 'When did you speak to Ryan and Rob?'

I was just blown away by the honour of it all. So many people were on that call, but these two new potential owners were talking about me – and not only speaking highly of my work but positioning me as key to their vision moving forward. I was highly respected by fans because I was doing a full-time job helping people for nothing. Now Ryan and Rob respected me, too, and were grateful for my endorsement.

James began to read through some of the questions: 'In 2018, WST members voted that the club meets agreed minimum standards of accessibility as soon as it's financially viable. As part of that, it was agreed to have a second wheelchair viewing platform. You mentioned speaking to Kerry already. The DSA is one of the schemes to support the football club. What are your intentions for potentially supporting them, going through the accessibility order that they've arranged?'

Rob picked up the thread. 'That's really one of our first calls,' he said. 'Within the first week, those are the exact kind of conversations we're going to be having. In terms of us coming up with the specifics of what *we* think it should be – I think that that's not the best way to go about it. I think we call Kerry, we speak with everybody on her end and on your end and we say: "What do you need?"'

My phone buzzed again: Mum. 'They've just mentioned you again!'

Back on the call, Ryan chipped in. 'That also really, to me, speaks to the kind of leadership – maybe I'm projecting – I would want if the roles were reversed. We're never going to be in a position where we're going to be shouting from the mountaintops that we know better than the Wrexham supporters or the infrastructure that is currently in place. We want to learn from that infrastructure. The thing I think we're both very good at is bolstering, helping – being the wind at your back. We want to really lean on those that know, and inclusivity is a huge part of what we do in our day jobs. It's something that's going to be of paramount importance going forward should this bid be accepted.'

I turned to Kings. 'I'm going to be able to have anything,' I breathed.

The whole time I'd worked at Wrexham, I'd always been searching for the next thing. The Trust always supported my ideas, but I'd been doing all the fundraising myself. These two were now telling me that they were going to back me all the way – that they were buying into what I was doing for disability and wanted to listen to my expertise. My thoughts raced with all of the things that would suddenly be possible.

Once Ryan and Rob logged off, the conversation turned to the fans' thoughts. Members had the opportunity to make statements for or against the proposed takeover, with each member allocated a maximum of five minutes to express their view.

The discussion was overwhelmingly positive. Many felt that Ryan and Rob were sincere. Hearing from them directly had had the desired effect, and people were relieved to have answers to all the rumours and conjecture. It didn't feel like Ryan and Rob were hiding anything, and that reassured people. Although there had been more than a thousand of us on the call, Ryan and Rob had a way of speaking that made you feel like they were talking to you directly.

Many felt like they had won the lottery: how had little Wrexham in North Wales, stranded outside league football for more than a decade and almost wiped off the face of the earth due to previous ownership, been handed this opportunity? If this worked, it gave us a really good chance of finally getting out of the National League.

It all seemed to move so quickly. We had gone from rumours to an announcement to a Zoom call to the world's press camping outside the Racecourse. There were cameras everywhere, lining the streets leading up to the entrances and clustering in the car park.

When we were collared by reporters, the golden rule was to tell them that we couldn't speak without prior permission from the media team. Even that was new: the club had never had to enforce anything like that because, simply put, no one ever asked to speak to us. Certainly no one from the national press, let alone international. Before Rob and Ryan appeared on the scene, I was often the one the media called for radio and television interviews because my work was always positive, improving access to the ground and far removed from the vagaries of what was happening on the pitch.

That meant that I had some experience of dealing with the press, and the media team started to call me at home to ask me if I could meet – either the next day or in a couple of hours – with broadcasters outside the club shop. From the corner of my eye, I would see the next camera crew pulling up, laying their cables and rigging their lights even before I'd finished the first interview. 'What's it like to work at Wrexham?' 'What do you think Ryan and Rob can bring?' I don't relish the attention, but it became normal in those days. The answers started to roll off the tongue.

Kings reassured me that I was doing a good job. He recorded my interviews on the Sky box and, when we later cancelled our subscription, set up a tripod and taped the TV live so that he wouldn't lose them. I never tried to put myself out there or to become the face of the club, but the requests kept coming. I sometimes felt a little bit guilty that other people didn't get more attention; instead, three different film crews would shoot me in front of three different parts of the ground.

The link arrived over email for all members of the Trust to cast their vote on whether Wrexham AFC should be sold to Ryan and Rob. For the sale to go through, they needed 75 per cent of members in favour of the motion.

I loved the Trust: the camaraderie, the way everybody could have their say and how we all felt part of something very special. People did things out of love and loyalty to the club, and not because they wanted to line their pockets. I had fallen in love with Wrexham under the WST, although I knew that a lot of the time it lived hand to mouth. Ryan and Rob brought the promise of better days – the chance that we could be something, could go places. And they weren't just making promises to the club, but to the whole of Wrexham. That this was during a pandemic, when every town and city had suffered so much economically, was also very powerful. In that respect, independent shop owners had as much to look forward to as football fans. I knew, too, that moving to a new ownership model would give us a far better chance of keeping our most special players and getting out of the National League. For me, my vote was a foregone conclusion.

Kings and I had cast our votes, but it felt like time trickled by as we waited to see how everyone else leaned. We were nervous to see the result, but confident the deal would go through. Like all Wrexham fans, we followed all the news channels for updates on the takeover. My dad spent hours each day ringing me to let me know that the club was being discussed on some show or other. 'I've just sat down for my dinner and this is on – make sure you change the channel!' It was constant, and the press never seemed to lose their enthusiasm for the story, nor run out of angles to cover. They'd be interviewing members of the public and speaking to local businesses. Then the call would come in from Dad: he'd spotted someone he knew.

During this time, I felt sorry for Rob because the focus was almost entirely on Ryan. That wasn't Ryan's fault, but I feel like Rob didn't get the credit he deserved until *Welcome to Wrexham* premiered. Then, fans were able to see that the idea of buying a football club had really started with him, and he'd been the driving force behind sealing the deal. I think the football world sees them as a pair now, instead of just tagging Rob on the end.

Then came the biggest update so far: the Wrexham Supporters Trust members had voted overwhelmingly in favour of Ryan and Rob. A whopping 98.6 per cent of us had said yes.

Every news channel ran the story, and we flicked between stations to take in the pictures of Ryan, Rob and the ground we knew so well. Later that evening, the coverage turned to the parties outside the ground. A local band, the Declan Swans, had released a song called 'Always Sunny in Wrexham', and this was the chant of choice for Wrexham fans out celebrating that night. 'No one's invested as much as a penny', it went. 'Bring on the Deadpool and Rob McElhenney!'

Kings and I looked at each other in disbelief as one fan dressed as Deadpool drove a Vespa past The Turf while fireworks exploded behind him. The town's reaction was so extreme, way beyond anything we could have anticipated.

That stunt still didn't inspire me to watch one of Ryan's films! Kings and Casey love action films, but I'm not very good at suspending my disbelief. I'm a bigger fan of Ryan's wife, Blake Lively, and her work. But we did watch *Always Sunny* from the beginning – which tuned out the sound of Casey telling me how it was all wasted on me!

Every day for months, we'd read reports of families losing their livelihoods and businesses shutting down because they'd been decimated by the loss of revenue in the pandemic. Those anxieties were then replaced by a buzz. Wrexham was the only town in the whole of the UK that had something to look forward to: the promises of Ryan and Rob.

# CHAPTER ELEVEN

# 'ALL CHANGE, PLEASE'

Ryan and Rob announced their takeover through a tongue-in-cheek advertisement for Ifor Williams, a North Walian trailer manufacturer.

'Not sure what to get your special one this holiday?' Rob began.

'Tired of them opening the same old scarf or sweater?' Ryan chimed in.

'Nothing says "I'm thinking of you" – or your horse – like an Ifor Williams Trailer.'

That was them all over: you had to laugh because they'd deliberately butchered the pronunciation and were gently making fun of the Welsh accent. It was an early taste of the marketing we would have to get used to, with the randomness of two Hollywood stars promoting a British trailer company not only reminding everyone of how wacky all this was but also subtly advertising the boost they'd give to brands who wanted to come on board.

'They're at it again!' Kings and I say to each other when things like that happen now. They have a tradition, for example, of outlandishly celebrating each other's birthdays. In 2022, a gold plaque appeared marking the Rob McElhenney Commemorative Urinal in one of the toilets at the Racecourse, which Ryan unveiled on social media with a video of him cutting a small ribbon and popping champagne; Rob returned the gift in kind later that year, launching the Ryan Reynolds Memorial Blimp from the centre circle on a matchday. In 2025, Ryan superimposed Rob into some of his old films as an apology for Rob's cameo in *Deadpool & Wolverine* not making the final cut.

There were delays to the takeover as the Financial Conduct Authority pored over the finer points of the deal. Ryan and Rob had to demonstrate that the sale of the club was in the best interests of the community, and this went on for so long that in the end the Football Supporters' Association had to come and help.

Some fans started to get a little bit jittery. Was it all going to collapse? Why was it taking so long? When Ryan and Rob put in some money for the January 2021 transfer window, we felt reassured: the takeover was delayed but not off completely. In fact, the takeover wasn't confirmed until 9 February, three months after the vote. They were waiting for a while before they could celebrate with the video for Ifor Williams.

To see our team and town mentioned in those kinds of social media posts and watch them blow up, the number of shares and comments rising by the second, was just bizarre. The strangest thing was seeing Ryan's celebrity friends posing in Wrexham shirts. The Canadian astronaut Chris Hadfield shared a photo of himself in a Wrexham jersey and face mask after a win over Yeovil. 'Beautiful win today, @Wrexham_AFC,' he tweeted. 'I hadn't watched much National League, but I suspect that's about to change. Great choice of team, Ryan.' More than three thousand people liked the post, and he replied to one fan telling them that he liked to watch matches in space. We had to get used to that: Jason Bateman and Will Arnett went on to wear Wrexham gear in posts in 2021.

We didn't quite get it at first, but then realised it was a marketing masterstroke. 'That's Ryan's way of subliminally getting the message out there without actually paying for a big advert,' Kings said in amazement. 'He's got another movie star to put on a top and people are commenting and making a fuss.'

Elsewhere, Wrexham staff were making social content of their own. In 2021, I suggested to the manager at the time, Dean Keates, that we do the viral Ice Foot 92 ice bucket challenge in aid of the Motor Neurone Disease Association. He was well up for it. When I rocked up with buckets of ice, the players were running around and threatening to splash me.

'You've got to do it!' they said to me as they stood up, shivering, from their stools.

'It won't be a problem for me because I'm paralysed in one leg,' I taunted, 'so I can't feel anything! Bring it on!'

They fell about laughing at the fact they'd been made to do it and couldn't even get their revenge on me. We made our donation to the charity on behalf of the club and posted the videos online.

At other times, Ryan and Rob's posts read like normal fans as they posted pictures of themselves streaming matches or commenting on performances.

Those streams of the matches improved. Shaun Harvey, the former chief executive of Leeds United, had been brought in as an adviser to the board (he was later made director). He spoke to Bryn Law, the Welsh football commentator, who helped to improve the club's streaming service and later surprised everyone when he appeared pitch side on the coverage of Wrexham vs Woking introducing the interviews with players and managers. Bryn was born and bred in my village, Ruabon, his parents living around the corner from mine, and he knew Shuan from their shared days at Leeds United.

Once fans were finally allowed into matches at the start of 2022, they found a changed, freshened-up Racecourse. There was suddenly the sound of clip-clopping around the stands: every woman sported a pair of high heels and was done up to the nines on match-days and out searching for a glimpse of Ryan Reynolds. I'm only half joking. Before, the Racecourse was welcoming, but it always felt like a man's domain. The minute Ryan and Rob arrived, the crowd filled with families – more than I'd ever seen in all my years going to the club. You heard accents from all around the world. It was refreshing to see kids out and about in Wrexham tops, having only ever seen local children wearing clobber from Premier League clubs. Crowds began to hang outside the gated entrances in the hope of catching Ryan, Rob and the players.

'Do you know how long they'll be?' the fans would ask Kings and me as we exited. 'Are they in there?' Sometimes it felt unfair to tell them that Ryan and Rob had already left or would still be another two hours because they had someone else to meet or were busy filming something. I felt a bit guilty that they had such a long wait in store for just a few seconds with the people I'd been spending time with.

Some older Wrexham fans would voice their frustrations with all these changes, complaining that they could no longer get tickets for matches or had to sit next to American fans who didn't understand football. When I heard comments like that, I always said the same thing: that we were all new fans once. It doesn't matter where they come from – every new fan should be welcomed.

The Racecourse had always been known for having a good following and a decent atmosphere, led largely by Jacko, who was also one of the lead singers of the Fron Male Voice Choir. He would always get the crowd going in his section. Sometimes it was hard for him to get chants to take off when there were so many empty seats, but he always tried his best until his passing in 2017. Following Ryan and Rob's takeover, though, different sections of the ground would start off the singing, and their words quickly rippled around the ground because the Racecourse was full.

New staff began to arrive: new heads of department, and, in some cases, heads of those heads. I had always known everyone at Wrexham, and they had always known me, but gradually the club began to fill with new faces.

Humphrey Ker was our conduit to Ryan and Rob at the very top of the club. He was a British actor who, viewers of *Welcome to Wrexham* would learn, had first introduced Rob to football and was instrumental in their decision to purchase Wrexham. For the next three years, Humphrey split his year exactly in half between Wrexham and the US, spending six months at a time in each. I like Humphrey, as he always wants the best for people, and generally left you to get on with the job you were good at and didn't interfere.

Fleur Robinson had previously worked as commercial director of Burton Albion under her father Ben, who was the club's chairman. She had been key to Burton's rise from non-league to the Championship. She started on 1 June 2021 as our new CEO. At Wrexham, she was abreast of everything and across every department, jumping from meeting to meeting and having the final sign-off before things went to Humphrey. Fleur put lots of trust in me and used to contact me often to ask for my view on things. I almost became one of her confidants, and that made me feel empowered in my role as DLO.

Fleur's right-hand woman was Julie, who had been a Gold Commander with the police at Brighton and Hove Albion Football Club. Can you believe that our accounts department used to consist of just one man? We had a new commercial manager, where previously we'd had two lads running the whole of the club shop and selling tickets.

Both those lads left, as did a few others who had been employed by the Trust but struggled to adapt to the new pace as the club turned into a more professional business. Many still have a relationship with Wrexham – some have season tickets, and Spencer Harris, for example, became honorary Vice President – but it's hard to explain the speed of change. Things didn't change just a little bit; they became unrecognisable overnight. The whole place had been run by volunteers, but that culture completely disappeared.

My volunteer DLO support DJ Povey has helped me since I started my role and supervises our Macron platform on match days. I wouldn't be able to do my job without him. In 2023, I put him forward for Volunteer of the Month with the National League, as someone had done for me once. DJ won, which was truly deserved. As of 2025, he is probably the only volunteer remaining at the club.

There were scores of new hires who came to Wrexham in the hope of having a hotline to Ryan Reynolds, only to find that working in football is far more demanding and unglamorous than most people think – with unsociable hours, no weekends and plenty of calls on your days off. Many of those people didn't see out their probation periods.

Among those who stayed were the club secretary, the stadium manager, the commercial manager, Chal the groundsman and me. It didn't cross my mind that they might want to replace me because they'd been so passionate about the work I'd done and keen to support me. Those were their exact words on the call. They'd been told I was someone they needed to get on board and I had been asked personally to come and work for them. At the end of every working day, I'd think: *This is mad. Stuff like this doesn't happen to little old Wrexham.*

It felt like the club was on fast-forward. Things felt topsy-turvy at times, and it was hard to get used to the revolving door of arrivals and departures. None of that was Ryan and Rob's fault; it was just the product of such a dramatic change in circumstances. There had been pressures and stresses working for the Trust, but never these kinds of demands on our time. There were targets and meetings and people calling to find out how far along you were with the work you'd been set. It was a very steep learning curve, and lots of talent-ed people understandably felt that their roles were unrecognisable from the ones they'd originally signed up for.

It started to settle down after the first twelve months, but work-ing culture and its pace remains one of the most dramatic chang-es that took place during Ryan and Rob's ownership. By the time we reached League One, they were recruiting staff from Premier League clubs and even further afield like Serie A. You should see some of the club names listed on the weekly email update intro-ducing us to new staff: Inter Milan, Liverpool. How does Wrexham attract people who have worked with those clubs? Ryan and Rob's reputations, and the promise of where they will take us all. Every department has quadrupled in size. The academy has gone from the work of ten people to the domain of more than seventy.

I joke that I wouldn't be able to get my own job because no one comes through the door now without a degree, experience at a top club or having been headhunted. Wrexham has become a rare case among football clubs in that its manager is one of the few constants.

It's given me a greater incentive to prove myself, and I'm proud that I have been part of the story since the very beginning.

Ryan and Rob's people insisted that we all undergo some media training: what we could say, how to present ourselves and, most importantly, what we could post on social media. The session was led by Byrn Law in the Centenary Club, who had trained lots of young players and aspiring football coaches on how to use social media in the most effective way. We'd never had anything like that before, which is why so much information used to be leaked about transfers. Fans enjoyed flaunting their insider information and they were always right. I would always try to shut down conversations that veered into that territory, even if I knew the information they were after.

All those conversations people had held so casually, at home and on the school run and in cafes and supermarkets, had extra significance now because people would have incentives to leak information to the press for money or followers or clout. Bryn explained how fatal it was when clubs responded to fans who had been goading them – even a joking reply could open a whole can of worms, and it rarely ended well. That was for clubs who were in the Premier League, and we had to get ready for that level of scrutiny.

He showed us examples to drive home the significance of what was about to happen: companies had drawn criticism because their employees had brought them into disrepute, as in the case of delivery drivers who had stopped to urinate up the walls of houses. 'Now, "Wrexham FC employee does something stupid" will also be a headline,' Bryn said. 'There is extra scrutiny on the club because of this new spotlight. You can't offer people the opportunity to jump on something bad connected with Wrexham. Your family members might also be linked to the club. You have less control over their accounts, but they could still cause issues.

'Wrexham itself is a brand, but the key thing is that Wrexham has now been taken over by two other significant brands in Rob and Ryan,' he continued. 'From now on, you are representing them. You are their employees. You might think that this is just a football club and that they've got lots and lots of businesses, but these are such high-profile individuals. Whether you like it or not, what you post reflects on them.' I took that to heart, and that message has always been in the back of my mind since that day.

Media attention was about to become part of life at the club. On that Zoom call with the fans, Ryan and Rob had confirmed the rumours that they would develop the documentary series that would become *Welcome to Wrexham*.

We realised that filming was already underway when we saw the cameras peeking in the frame of the Zoom call, but Ryan and Rob's own cameras then began arriving at the club, documenting the players every day and following the manager around.

You couldn't miss them. Suddenly, we were part of a massive production every single day, with camera crews setting up in offices and the changing room and crews milling about the car park. You were working on a film set. Our matchday meetings now covered where the cameras would be located for the filming crew. You would see them moving in and out of the club shop, filming supporters buying shirts. Each day, you never knew when they would turn up or if you were going to be filmed. It took so much getting used to.

Back then, we just thought that would only be for a few weeks, not years. We'd catch up with the film crew and they would tell us that they had spent a day at Paul Mullin's or Luke Young's house.

We'd see them follow the players out to training and record them having their dinner. We didn't have any idea what it would grow into – or that they'd be looking for staff to be part of their footage.

'We've got a spare couple of hours; can we come over?' they began to say to the staff. 'You're somebody else that we haven't done any filming with – are you available?'

All of us working at the club were blown away by how different this all was to what we had known pre-Ryan and Rob. The excitement about who would be filmed next grew by the day. Plenty were suspicious in the beginning and many weren't keen at all because they didn't know what the final product would look like. We hadn't seen any final edits. What would become of all this footage? What were we getting involved with? They became very aware of the presence of the cameras.

Very few staff members had been filmed when they first approached me. I always say the media isn't interested in *me*, but the impact that my work on accessibility has. But I put my own appointment with the film crew off for ages. Doctors had warned me about how seriously I had to take the pandemic, so when the *Welcome to Wrexham* crew first reached out to me I told them that Kings and I simply couldn't have people in the house. They were respectful but made it clear that they wanted to film me before they left. We kept in touch.

Eventually, the messages changed: 'If we don't film you now, we won't get you on the series.'

By the time we finally let them in, they had banked hours and hours of footage. I was the final person on their list before they started to pull the episodes together – we really did leave it until the eleventh hour. I was filled with dread not only because of the risks of the pandemic but because, despite my experience, I hated the attention that came with being filmed. Most of all I hated the un-known. The crew didn't give me any information about what they wanted to do or even what they wanted to talk about. All I knew was that they were desperate to film with me, and I didn't want to miss the chance to showcase all we do for accessibility and inclusion at our club. There was no better opportunity than this.

We all tested for Covid each week, including on the day of filming. Once everyone had the all-clear, the crew arrived in huge vans with blacked-out windows. Kings and I watched as they put cameras and lights outside our front window to mimic sunlight. Past them we could see the neighbours poking their heads out to see what was going on.

Then the film crew came in, wearing face masks. They began pull-ing out the sofas, rearranging the furniture. They wanted the dog to be filmed. They wanted the cat to be filmed. They wanted the tortoise to be filmed. None of those shots would make the final edit, but they were banking footage.

'One of those sofas will have to come out,' they said. 'There's not enough room.' Kings and I laughed.

'No, no – we mean it.'

'You are having a laugh,' I replied, shaking my head.

'What do you mean?'

'Do you know how much cleaning I've done in preparation for you coming over? But I haven't cleaned under that sofa!'

They carried the sofa out into our hallway. Panicked, I waved for Kings's attention and pointed at the black line of dust that had col-lected on the skirting board. 'Clean that! Quick!'

Miloš Balać, the co-executive producer, had spotted a picture of Casey in her Year 11 school photo – one she'd always hated because her hair was so curly.

'That'll be perfect to have behind you,' he said.

'Casey will absolutely die!' I insisted. 'There's no way you can use that picture. Can you use another one?' I sighed with relief as Miloš combed through the family pictures and found a replacement.

They spent a good few hours at our home that day. We discussed my backstory, how I'd started to volunteer at the club, why my job meant so much to me and all that I provided for disabled fans at Wrexham AFC. It was a wonderful opportunity. *Why had I got in such a state?* I remember thinking as I started to loosen up and enjoy the experience.

Miloš said that the team would come back on the morning of the next home game. They did, and filmed me putting on my coat, checking my paperwork and getting into the van. They rode with us, filming us the whole way as Kings and I had to make conversation about the match. They filmed us from behind, walking down the concourse and discussing my working day.

Then they pieced it all together and ran a full thirty-minute episode that would be shown all around the world.

• • •

In November 2016, thanks largely to the DSA, Wrexham became the first Welsh club to earn dementia-friendly status through our new initiatives such as our reminiscence group and dementia training for staff.

I'm very big on getting in touch with people and organisations to hear their thoughts on how we can improve the club. The advice of the people I worked with at the Alzheimer's Society was that you're never, ever totally dementia-friendly; it's something you always have to be working towards, by constantly improving things.

I became a Dementia Friend myself, for which I completed some training to get a good understanding of what dementia is. I went on another course through Glyndwr University to be a Dementia Friends Champion (now known as Ambassadors) so that I could run the training sessions myself for the club's Dementia Friends. I was invited onto the committee for Dementia Friendly Wrexham, a dedicated group of people who help organisations achieve dementia-friendly status and provide training and raise awareness within the community, because of my position at the club. As the Alzheimer's Society had emphasised, though, we could always be doing more.

In the close season of 2021, when there are no matches, I recruited a group of people living with all different types of dementia to come to the club and audit our facilities. I took them on a tour and asked them to point out to me anything at all that would improve their matchday experience.

There was such variety in the experiences of those eight people, and they highlighted things that I'd never even thought of. Our loos, for example, were all white: white walls, white toilets, white sinks. Two of the people on this tour had said they couldn't see the toilet or the sink. They explained that, as their condition had progressed, they could no longer distinguish between things when they were all the same colour. Thanks to their feedback, we painted the walls red – and it made all the difference to them.

Others said that they couldn't see steps. Instead they saw a hole and, worried they would fall into it, would try to jump it. That's why most clubs paint the edges of their stairs yellow. I reached out to a company for a quote for doing this in one stand. They came back to me with a figure of £10,000. That wasn't in my budget and the club didn't want an army of volunteers with paintbrushes having free rein of the place, but I proposed recruiting six trusted volunteers and supervising them each day as they painted the steps yellow and the nosings (the edge) black.

That's what we did, and Kings, of course, was among the volunteers. Joining him were Dilwyn, a maintenance operative at Wrexham who worked nights at the local hospital and back then was also our head steward; Matt, a volunteer with the ground staff; and Darren, a friend of Matt's. They started at 10 a.m. and finished by 4 p.m. Every Friday, as a treat, I bought bacon and sausage baps from Wayne's butty van at The Turf as a 'thank you'.

My other big project that year – and why I'd caught the attention of the film crew – was powerchair football. I discovered it through a post on Facebook. An organisation linked with disabilities was looking for new premises. 'It needs to be a place with storage facilities for powerchairs', they had written.

*Powerchair football? What's that?* I wondered. A quick internet search brought up the answer. Powerchair football is football adapted for wheelchair users, using an oversized ball and a specially designed form of electric wheelchair called a powerchair. These reach much higher speeds, spin to generate power and are fitted with metal foot guards that allow players to pass and dribble the ball. The sport is played inside because players are often vulnerable and the powerchairs need to be kept dry.

'I've got to bring this to Wrexham,' I said to Kings. Very few sports are open to wheelchair users, many of whom feel like exercise is closed off to them. I knew from my own experiences that people in wheelchairs write themselves off, on top of which society makes them think that they can't play sports or be part of something like that. Well, actually, you can.

I'd found something that full-time wheelchair users could enjoy.

They could be part of a team – and that could be transformative for them. We could also be the very first powerchair football team in Wales.

I started to pull together a proposal for the club: what powerchair football was, what it would cost, the requirements we'd need to meet and why we needed to do it. Via Fleur, the proposal went to Humphrey.

He emailed me to say that Ryan and Rob had asked how much money I needed. They suggested that the club would cover all the costs for powerchair up to a particular limit, and would commit to repairs, storage and the hire of the sports hall each week. But I knew that we could use that money more effectively.

I replied to Humphrey: 'Please, I don't want you to even consider this amount of money. We don't know if this will take off or if anybody will want to play it. The last thing I want to do is put £50,000–£60,000 into a new venture that drums up no interest.'

I reached out to a contact called Paul Gorman from the independent Leeds Powerchair FC. Their set-up was phenomenal: teams for different age groups and skill levels, training several times a week and competing in elite to beginner leagues. I also travelled to Liverpool and watched sessions at Greenbank to learn the rules.

Powerchair football is really hard work, and very much a skill that players have to hone over time. It's mentally exhausting because it demands such a high level of concentration. I very much doubt anyone takes to powerchair football immediately, in part because it can feel quite removed from football – the rules are very different – but also because some players have never used an electric wheelchair before. That's a whole learning curve in itself. We welcome anyone with a disability, so a powerchair was totally new to ambulant-disabled players.

As luck would have it, Paul from the Leeds club was replacing their powerchairs and willing to sell them to us at a cut price. He would give us twelve powerchairs for £2,000. People who play top-level powerchair football might pay in excess of £12,000 for their chairs, but I was finding some online for £4,000–£6,000 a chair. I expected that we'd need more than ten for our teamwork training sessions, as there are four players on a team, but we'd need subs, too.

'Because I have the opportunity to get these chairs, let's get the club set up and see what happens before we start looking at up-grades,' I told Humphrey.

Kings and I hired a van with a tail lift. Kings, who had a licence to drive vehicles up to three and a half tonnes from his working life as a delivery driver, lifted me into the passenger seat and we drove more than two hours to Leeds to load up the powerchairs.

Another powerchair football club in Liverpool was closing down and they had chairs to give us, too. We then were donated a hoist by our local Ableworld store which would be used to transfer our players into the powerchairs. Paul had put me in touch with Adam McEvoy, now the head coach of the Powerchair England squad, and he came down to Wrexham to lead the training session for our community foundation coaches (previously Wrexham AFC Com-munity Trust).

'Why aren't you doing the training?' Adam asked me.

'I don't need to be a powerchair football coach,' I said. 'I've got no football coaching qualifications.'

'It makes no difference,' he said. 'You can still do the training.' And that's how we got started.

We had leaflets made and delivered to St Christopher's School and Wrexham Artificial Limb and Appliance Centre at Wrexham

Maelor Hospital. I ran advertisements on the club website and in the local newspaper.

Word spread, and the bulk of the interest came from disabled Wrexham fans. Very quickly, we had around fifteen players who were raring to go for the launch in September 2021.

It would take Kings two hours to unload the powerchairs and drive them up to Wrexham University and two hours to put them away again. Kings would unload them single-handedly. Like all my ideas, this was my baby, but I wouldn't be able to do it without Kings, who would also be the one repairing and tweaking the chairs during the session. Powerchair football has had precisely the impact I'd anticipated. Some of the people who come to the club don't work or don't have a great social life. But every single Friday, they become part of a team, mix with people, build camaraderie and celebrate their successes. Some of our players are nonverbal and beep their horns in celebration when they score goals. It's exactly the kind of inclusivity I'd wanted when I established the club. As I'd written in my proposal: anyone who wants to come and play powerchair football should be able to.

Kings and I ran the club for three years before it moved under the control of Wrexham AFC Foundation. During that time, the club played a friendly at Manchester City and got to stay for a tour of the training facilities and to watch a Premier League match afterwards. At another friendly at Green Bank, the team played against one girl whose skills were out of this world, and she now plays in one of the top leagues. That was amazing for our players to experience because it gave them something to aspire to. When we first set up our powerchair football team, however, we still hadn't met Ryan and Rob.

# CHAPTER TWELVE

# RYAN AND ROB COME TO VISIT

At 4 p.m., the email arrived: 'Tomorrow, you'll all be meeting Ryan and Rob. They're coming.'

The final email of the working day was the most momentous and shrouded in the kind of secrecy that meant they were telling us all at the eleventh hour in case the news somehow got out. Fleur had attached Ryan and Rob's itinerary for the next few days: tours of key places, visits with significant people, boardroom meetings, when they would be having drinks.

Along with the rest of the club's staff, I would be meeting them at 11 a.m. I had to be there early in full uniform. I scanned the rest of the email and realised there was a section on protocol: do not ask for autographs, do not ask for pictures and do not speak to them unless they speak to you. Genuinely, it was like royalty was coming to visit.

To the surprise of the fans, Ryan and Rob had been to Maidenhead earlier that week to watch Wrexham in person for the first time. It was a total secret until just before the match started, when news started to spread on social media. Ryan posted on Instagram afterwards that football was a 'soul-deadening, evil and gorgeous game'. People had wondered when Ryan and Rob would begin to come to matches and now they were. Everything started to fall into place.

'Kings!' I shouted, calling him through from the other room. I called Dad and put him on loudspeaker, telling them the news at the same time.

•  •  •

As my full-time companion, Kings is always by my side. That means that he helps me to execute all my plans but also gets invited to lots of things that other partners don't. This time, though, felt a bit different. We were conscious that no other staff members had their families with them for what was a crucial introduction to our new employers, and Kings took the decision to wait in the car. 'Good luck!' he said, sending me on my way. 'Call me if you need me.'

Fleur's email had told us that we would have to arrive at the club for Covid tests at 10 a.m. That was the most anxious part of the day. People were pacing, fidgeting and checking their phones. What if their test came back positive? They wouldn't be meeting anybody then. For some, this would be their only chance to see Ryan and Rob. I didn't know at the time that I would see them every time they visited; some staff haven't been as lucky, not only because their paths have never crossed but because they're reticent to approach people they see as such big stars.

'It'll be my luck – just you watch,' I said as we waited. 'Mine will be positive.'

Then came the all-clear.

We were told to form a line on the far side of the pitch and stand, as though awaiting a royal visit, at intervals on the front row. I was the last in line, almost in the tunnel because I couldn't manoeuvre my wheelchair around the step. Then there was nothing to do but wait for the new bosses to show. Anything in football involves a lot of waiting around, and as people's legs started to ache, they moved up into the stands to sit down. My nerves started to build, and with them came the anxiety that something might go wrong and I might need to call Kings. All the while, he was in the car, watching TV on his phone. I'm not sure how much attention he paid to whatever he'd downloaded, but after thirty or forty minutes, he started to wonder where I was. Had I met them? Was I still waiting? Were we in the middle of a big conversation?

Every few minutes Fleur poked her head around the tunnel and we'd startle, thinking this was the big moment. 'No,' she'd say. 'Not ready yet.'

I had an advantage on most staff in that I'd already spoken to Rob, and in a small way, that calmed my nerves. People asked me what Rob had been like, and I thought back to that first call: my voice shaking and how quickly Rob had put me at ease when he'd spoken to me like we'd known each other for years. In return, I didn't feel overawed, so I spoke to him with a candour that he probably appreciated. Through my brother's career as an actor, Kings and I had met scores of famous people – soap and TV stars – but never anyone on this level.

After ninety minutes, we saw movement in the front car park: a fleet of chauffeur-driven vans with blacked-out windows. Figures emerged, then retreated to speak to the fans clamouring at the gate. We made out Rob in the black Wrexham cap that was his signature piece at that time, and with them was Humphrey.

Ryan and Rob arrived with a ring of cameramen, pausing to drink it all in. They broke off from the pack to walk to the centre circle. Ryan stood a moment, pondering the view, before flopping to the ground, his arms and legs spread into a star shape. He looked up at the sky and exhaled loudly, before picking a blade of grass and tucking it in his pocket. Then he took a call from his family, spinning around to capture the stadium for them.

He and Rob had only ever seen the Racecourse Ground from behind a screen, just as Ryan's family were doing now. Now that they were finally here they were overwhelmed by the stadium's size and the emotion of the moment – a reunion of sorts after being separated by a pandemic and thousands of miles for their entire tenure.

The staff laughed with them while also clocking the camera crew that were tracking Ryan and Rob and the boom mics and cameras flanking them as they made each step. That was striking then, but we've since all had to get used to them. Every interaction, no matter how small, is documented, just in case it becomes TV gold.

As they came over to start greeting the staff, they shouted out in front of everyone: 'Hey, Kerry!' From our earlier chat, they felt that they already knew me, but of course every other head swivelled to turn to me – the only time anyone had taken their eyes off the club's new owners. I was mortified, part of me still uncomfortable with the attention after all these years.

I watched intently as Ryan and Rob moved along our line. Fleur made the introductions, and we strained our ears to catch the swift exchanges and the pleasantries. 'What do you do? How long have you worked here?' Hands were shaken. 'That's fantastic.' They complimented Chal on the state of the pitch, glad to see a return on their investment after putting money into the playing surface. Then it was my turn.

'Hey, Kerry!' Rob said again. 'Nice to finally meet you in person.'

'How you doing, Kerry?' asked Ryan. 'You good?'

They each threw their arms around me and hugged me.

Fleur went to make the introductions, but Ryan chimed in. 'We already know Kerry.'

Fleur brought up the powerchair football club – they said that they were looking forward to coming to see us the next night – and the Quiet Zone, while I explained what my work as a volunteer involved and how many hours I dedicated, unpaid, to the club.

'You did all this as a volunteer?' Rob said in amazement. 'You do an absolutely amazing job. We can't wait to work with you. Anything at all you need, you only have to say.'

They asked me if I had enough space for the Quiet Zone and if I wanted to look at expanding it. I knew where they were coming from: if the space was three times the size it is now, I have no doubt we'd be able to fill it. I have a waiting list and sadly have to turn so many people away because there isn't room to house them all without compromising the attention we give the families we already host. My view has always been that we wouldn't be able to maintain that level of engagement in a bigger space.

'Although that section has 165 seats, we probably have about 130 people coming,' I explained. 'We try to leave room between each family. We have specific stewards who look after that area and it's all under my care. Those stewards have conversations with the families, help those who are struggling. We couldn't give them that kind of TLC if the area was twice the size.'

Ryan and Rob also offered me a glass box in the middle of the stand as a sensory room, and again I declined. 'The kids can't trudge through the stand, up the stairs and past all the noisy fans on the concourse to go to a sensory room,' I said. 'Although ours is small, it's perfect because it's right at the back of our area. The kids know their way there. They know there will be no fans there. They know everything about it. If you're a child who needs to use a sensory room, you're not going to be able to cope with wading through a stand of 2,000 people.'

They completely understood. 'You know best,' they said. 'We just want to ensure that you've got what you need.'

After our conversation, they were whisked up the tunnel to see the changing rooms, the next calling point on a whistle-stop tour of the club and town that would also, at various points, take in Spencer Harris's house, a nightcap at The Turf with Wayne and my power-chair football club on Friday night.

Before that stop, though, they had to navigate a press conference with the world's media, as well as fans who had been invited to apply for tickets to a Q&A with Ryan and Rob. Those who had been successful in the ballot had been posting on social media about how they couldn't believe their luck.

Some staff members were invited along by the club, and I was among them. It reflected my standing at the club at that stage, but I still felt as though I didn't need telling twice. Kings and I watched from the accessible viewing platform alongside Shaun Harvey and a handful of staff as Ryan and Rob greeted the assembled media in the Macron stand.

Kings and I both had different concerns going into the press conference. Like most Wrexham fans, Kings's only experience with Ryan and Rob had been in that initial Zoom call with 1,300 fans. He had liked them, but a part of him was still unsure whether to take them at face value because they were, after all, both actors. Other fans felt the same. Were Ryan and Rob being themselves? Were they genuine? In the press conference, he wanted to see honesty, see them wearing their hearts on their sleeves.

By his own admission, Ryan wasn't necessarily the biggest soccer or football fan when he first bought Wrexham, but he has since fallen in love with the game. In that respect, his journey with the club is similar to mine. Maybe that's why my chief preoccupation was with whether any of the Wrexham fans would make themselves look foolish on TV. Before Ryan and Rob came, the town and its people hadn't often had a chance to show themselves off. Kings and I were always rooting for people on quiz shows and news broadcasts when they introduced themselves as being from Wrexham but then cringing when they put their feet in their mouths.

Kings turned to Shaun. 'Don't you find this a bit bonkers?' he asked.

'No, not really. It's a bit different, but it's not bonkers,' was all Shaun said.

Kings turned back to me and gave me a look that said: *No – this really is bonkers.*

That's typical Shaun – he tells it exactly how it is and everything just rolls off him. He'd been similarly unaffected when one day in mid-June a horsebox was deposited in the middle of the Racecourse car park and all the gates locked. Security was on all the entrances, not allowing anyone access.

To look at Shaun's relaxed, jovial demeanour, you wouldn't think that arguably the biggest sponsors in the club's history were preparing a landmark commercial shoot with all the players. The set-up was angled so that no one in the surrounding student flats would be able to see in, with the players ushered into the horsebox so that they could record in private. This was the biggest secret going, but Kings and I were in the car park, stood out of the way, with Shaun, catching up and watching the film crews at work.

About a week later, the club announced that the sponsor was TikTok. A sponsor that size was unheard of for a club at our level.

That Kings and I had witnessed their arrival was special but also a strange moment – probably the last instance of informality around big productions like that before club business became more private. No one had thought to usher Kings and me out of there, but we wouldn't be allowed anywhere near that kind of thing now.

Back at the press conference, talk had turned – in a way – to Ryan's day job. 'If this was a movie,' one reporter asked, 'what would be your perfect ending?'

'I'd be lying if it wasn't Premier League or something like that,' Ryan said, 'but this is a long road.'

There was the headline, and the other journalists smelled it. Another reporter mentioned that Ryan and Rob could have bought a Premier League club instead and got an instant seat at football's top table. He asked if they like a challenge.

'You realise you started by saying we're gonna take Wrexham to the Premier League – and they all recorded it?' Rob replied.

'That is the goal, isn't it?' Ryan said.

'That's the way we've been talking about it all the way through,' Rob said. 'Maybe this is my own naivete, but I would say to Humphrey: "The way that the system works… couldn't we theoretically get to the Premier League?" And he sort of laughed and said: "Well, yes, but that would never happen." And I don't understand why, if you can theoretically get there. We clearly have the structure and the system, potentially, to allow for us to grow at that scale. Why not dream big?'

'If you don't think like that, I don't think you'll ever go there,' Ryan concluded.

Kings and I jerked to attention. He gave me a look as if to say: *This is getting a bit ridiculous.* We had been in the National League for fifteen years. Just getting out of there would be something. In recent years, you couldn't see anything beyond a relegation to National League North. Where had this talk of the Premier League come from? We just took their words with a pinch of salt.

Later on, playing their words back, it dawned on us: Ryan and Rob are fascinated by the promotion and relegation system in the English leagues. American sports are all closed leagues, with no movement up and down at the end of each season. All the talk since they had arrived had focused on getting out of the National League, but this aspect of English football appealed to them from the off – so why wouldn't they want to take us all the way? Their resources and investment meant that they could make it all real.

• • •

On Friday, Kings and I prepared to welcome Ryan and Rob to the powerchair football club.

We'd had the same sort of briefing as the day before. We were told how we could speak to them, that everyone at the club had to sign waivers giving their consent to be filmed and that Ryan and Rob would spend no longer than ten minutes with us. Most crucially, if word got out about the visit, the whole thing would be off. The last thing they needed was thousands of fans descending on the sports hall and causing a safety issue.

I had to pass all this on to the players, who understandably wanted to bring everyone they knew along with them. They felt so privileged to be meeting the new owners on Ryan and Rob's very first visit to the club – and that Ryan and Rob were coming to powerchair football before they'd even watched a match at the Racecourse.

'You bring the carer you normally come with, but you can't turn up with half your family,' I said to each player. 'If this gets out, no one will get to see them. You have to keep this hushed.'

As players and carers waited for the results of their Covid tests, I took a briefing from the filming crew, who wanted the team to keep playing as Ryan and Rob walked in so that they could get footage of the practice. None of us wanted the players to rush over to Ryan and Rob and for that reaction to be the story when there was an opportunity to showcase their skills and hard work. I told them instead to show off what they could do. We'd only started the club a month earlier, but they looked good and had made so much progress in that short space of time. Of course, the contrast between how they played then and how they play now is night and day, but no one knew any different back then.

To their credit, the team did exactly what we'd asked them to when forty people entered the sports hall. Ryan and Rob were somewhere among the crowd, surrounded by a full camera crew, Wrexham's media team, their bodyguards and whoever else was in their entourage. Inevitably, a few players sneaked a glance out of the corner of their eye, but that was it.

I went to the door of the sports hall to meet Ryan and Rob. They stood on either side of me as I explained what powerchair football was and how the rules differed from conventional football, thinking we only had ten minutes to get all of this across to the film crew.

They stayed for over an hour.

Powerchair football is an intense, immersive sport that bears such a resemblance to football but breaks so much new ground. Players swivel and spin to generate power, and the clanging and banging of a crunching tackle is like watching bumper cars slamming into each other. The best team moves require intense concentration and speed of thought, and when all that comes together, the sport is hugely impressive. It's no wonder Ryan and Rob were swept up in it.

'Go on!' they shouted, cheering incisive moves and goals and tackles. The passion rolled off them in waves. I don't think they expected what they saw, or maybe they didn't even have a concept of what they were going to experience. Powerchair football hooks people in quickly, and perhaps that took them by surprise. In any case, our players and coaches hadn't planned to put on a full session – the whole point of this meeting was to give Ryan and Rob a five-minute demo. But they showed no sign of leaving, so on it went. I could see our players lighting up with the attention from their adoring audience.

'How long before they'll be able to compete?' Ryan asked.

'Give us a chance – we've only just started,' I said jokingly, explaining that there would be leagues that we could enter, as well as international tournaments. I added that we were the first powerchair football team in Wales, which Ryan found especially impressive.

'No pressure,' he said. 'I want Kerry to run my whole company. She's killing it out here.'

All the while, Ryan stood and chatted to us like we'd known him forever. We talked about how I never thought I'd work again, how Andy and Macclesfield had sown a seed and I'd wanted Wrexham to have an Andy of their own, how the job had snowballed into something bigger than I could have anticipated. I explained how important the job was in giving me a sense of self again and the role it had played in restoring my confidence.

'I owe everything to Wrexham,' I said to them.

'No, we owe everything to you,' replied Rob.

After about forty-five minutes, Rob called his son. He held out his arm and turned in a slow circle, trying to capture everything.

'What's this, Dad?' came the voice from the other end of the phone call.

'This is one of our teams at Wrexham,' said Rob. 'Wait 'til you come to the club and you can watch this.'

A tinny voice squeaked back: 'Cool!'

That moment was just so special because, straight away, Rob included the powerchair football players alongside the men's and women's teams. I'll never forget that.

'I hope you don't mind me asking, but what is cerebral palsy and what happened?' asked Ryan.

I explained how I had been mobile throughout my childhood and lost the ability to walk after my cerebral bleed. Ryan was listening intently, rather than just nodding out of habit – you could tell because he would ask relevant questions. Out of the corner of my eye, I could see the cameras. I never hide what happened to me – I can't – but I remember thinking that this was a very personal conversation to be having with a boom mic hanging over me. But Ryan seemed to genuinely care, and that was reassuring.

He asked how Kings and I had met, and Kings told him the story: how we'd been friends for years and that he'd asked me out hundreds of times but I'd always turned him down. 'What was *wrong* with you, Kerry?' Ryan gasped. 'Why did you make this man wait? He's lovely. He's got lovely eyes.' Ryan understood when I said that I didn't want to ruin the friendship, and we discussed the relatives I had out in Canada.

I had been to Vancouver in my teens. Mum and Dad had paid for my ticket out there and for their troubles got a call from my auntie fretting about why everyone else had come through arrivals and I was still nowhere to be seen two hours after the plane had landed. Immigration suspected that I had run away from home and had interviewed me. 'Run away from home?' I remember saying, incredulously. 'If I did run away from home, I'd have run to Joanne, not all the way to Canada!' In the end, after I'd endured a grilling from several different staff and watched them empty my luggage, they walked me through to my auntie and uncle. They had to pass over their details and fill in forms detailing how they knew me. This all tickled Ryan, who thought I must have looked young to endure all of that at the airport. I ended up loving my time with Auntie Gwyn and Uncle Glyn so much that I thought of moving to Canada. I got a job offer as a nanny, but I'm too much of a home bird, so I declined it. My auntie and uncle were a massive part of my childhood, and I adored them like another Nan and Granddad. They have both passed now, but I keep in contact with their family.

Sometimes people feel intimidated by Ryan – not because of anything he does, but because of his star power and the size of his public profile. They are wary of approaching him and hesitant to speak with him, but I can honestly say that all of our conversations have felt familiar and never awkward. He had greeted me on Thursday like an old friend, and at powerchair football I found him so easy to talk to. He filled the conversation with genuine warmth, asking all the questions, and I felt like I could have been talking to anyone.

I found them both respectful, too, of the club and what it stood for. A member of the film crew asked Ryan and Rob if they wanted footage of them in the chair and playing themselves. They both declined, and I respected them for that. I sometimes see people playing on wheelchairs, leaning back and riding on two wheels, trying to skid around corners as fast as they can. I find that disrespectful because wheelchairs aren't toys. They're not to giggle at or mess about on.

'No,' Ryan said to his crew, 'because I can get in and out of the chair. I don't want anyone to think that we're taking the mick out of people in wheelchairs.'

Ryan pulled Kings, Rob and I in for a picture to mark his visit to powerchair football before they both then turned and spoke to the group, telling the players that they were hugely impressed by their skills and looked forward to hearing about their progress. They had a photo with the team in the centre circle and invited everyone to ask for pictures and autographs. We staff had been told that it was inappropriate to ask for those things – at the end of the day, Ryan and Rob were our bosses – but in this instance, they had offered.

'I can't believe this,' I said to Kings while we waited our turn. 'We met them yesterday. We were told they'd stay for ten minutes at powerchair football but they've been here an hour. And the depth of conversation!'

Kings had a copy of that weekend's programme that he wanted signed, which had Ryan and Rob on its cover. He'd taken the first one out of the box when they'd been delivered to the club earlier that week. But the pen Kings had was a whiteboard marker, not a permanent one. 'Is it going to be all right?' Ryan said. 'You'll have to blow on it. I'm here again tomorrow. I'll redo it for you if it smudges.'

We keep it upstairs on display. And, yes, it survived the journey home.

'See you tomorrow, Kerry,' Rob called as they left the room. In five seconds, the place emptied. But then the noise started. Our players had been on their best behaviour all evening, but now they could let out the excitement. But my brain had caught on to what Rob had just said. *Tomorrow?* 'Yes,' Fleur said, stopping on her way out and turning to me. 'Tomorrow, I want you to be part of the unveiling with them on the Wrexrent platform.'

In 2021, the club had received a grant of £400,000 from the Premier League through the Football Stadia Improvement Fund to create a second viewing platform for disabled fans (the first was built back in 2015 with support from the DSA, Wrexham AFC and Glyndwr University, as it was then known). It was located in the Wrexrent (now the STōK Cold Brew Coffee) stand, behind the goal nearest to the university.

I've always hated that while able-bodied fans can choose where they sit at football grounds, wheelchair users are almost always put on the front row. I said to the club that the one thing that we need to create for wheelchair users at Wrexham was choice: sitting behind the goal with the drummer would never be my dream, but some people want to be part of that atmosphere, and it would be wrong to deny them that.

Another issue is that most clubs assign companions a seat on the row behind the wheelchair user. That perplexes me. When you go with your friend to a football match, do you buy your seats one behind the other? Of course not – you sit together. What if the wheelchair user is nonverbal? How do they get the attention of the people behind or in front of them? I've always made sure that our companion seats are at the side of our wheelchair users.

I had been part of the planning for the platform, which was why Fleur had invited me to be part of its unveiling. Our thoughts then turned to the next day. What would happen, with a stadium of almost 10,000 fans, when we had to cut the ribbon – when I would, in my own way, be in the middle of it all?

I arrived at the Racecourse on Saturday morning to find Fleur clutching a pair of giant gold scissors. 'You're in charge of getting these,' she said, handing them to me, 'over there.' She pointed to the new wheelchair viewing platform. 'Hand them to Ryan and Rob when it's time to cut the ribbon.'

I felt the weight of them in my lap. 'Are you having a laugh?' I replied in astonishment. 'Have you seen the size of them? How do I get these into a stadium and past security and the police?'

'Well, if you're not in position by 2.30 p.m., we'll send out a search party and assume you've been arrested.'

While they would usually watch the game from their box and arrive long before everyone else, Rob and Ryan being pitch side, on a slightly raised platform surrounded by fans, on their very first home game at the Racecourse, was always going to inspire a very intense reaction among supporters, particularly after they'd addressed the fans from the centre circle.

'We just wanted to say thank you so much to this community for opening up your arms to us these last few days,' Ryan said into the microphone. 'It means the absolute world to us. We're so grateful.'

'*Diolch yn fawr!*' shouted Rob. *Thank you very much.*

I could hear the fans screaming for Ryan and Rob, climbing over each other for better views and photos. I stood at one end of the ribbon in front of the media team and cameras, the throng of press three rows deep. I'd told Dad to come down to that end of the ground so that he could see what was going on, but he told me later on that he hadn't been able to see anything because the crowds were so thick. On and on the chanting went.

That reaction to Ryan and Rob has never changed in their whole time at the club. I absolutely hate close crowds: if you're lower down in a wheelchair and people are packed in at either side of you, it's hard to gauge their movements and it feels intimidating and unsafe. This was the only time I'd ever felt a flicker of anxiety at the club – the one place where I'm always unaffected because it feels like home to me. The people there are my normal. The Racecourse is my normal. Entering into Ryan and Rob's world would be a bit of an adjustment.

I waited at one end of the ribbon beside Ryan, Rob and two wheelchair users we'd invited to be part of the unveiling. We chatted, and Ryan and Rob expanded on the themes of our first conversation, expressing their gratitude for all I had done and their astonishment that I'd done it all with no budget and as a volunteer. Then came an unexpected turn.

'We'd like to thank you for all you've done for us,' Rob said, 'and for you to come on board with us as a full-time member of staff.'

Ryan nodded in agreement. 'We've had conversations with Fleur. Everything is in place. What do you think?'

'Wow,' I gasped. 'Thank you so much.'

What followed, as the cameras assembled and the countdown began, was my favourite interaction with Ryan. I'm lucky that the very moment was captured for posterity, and the picture, which I've included in this book, shows Ryan leaning towards me and my bottom lip trembling. It's such an unflattering picture of me that anyone who sees it without understanding the context will wonder why I've kept hold of it. But talk about a picture speaking a thousand words. When people ask me what really stands out since the Hollywood takeover, it's this – and Ryan Reynolds, of all people, telling me: 'Kerry, if my girls grow up to be anything like you, I'll be the proudest dad alive.'

# CHAPTER THIRTEEN

# WEMBLEY

My planning for Wrexham's trip to Wembley for the 2022 FA Trophy Final began before the semi-final that got us there.

I'd been thinking throughout that cup run about the possibility of running a Quiet Zone bus. What would that involve, and who would I have to contact? What would we need? Some people in the Quiet Zone go to lots of away games now, but many don't, and going all the way to London to watch a game in an unfamiliar stadium would be a totally different – and daunting – experience. We'd need access to a sensory room, a vantage point similar to the one they have at Wrexham, all the tickets seated together and a designated bus – I'd have to message Pat's Coaches – and I'd need to clear all of this with Wembley before I even mentioned it to the parents. I didn't want to make promises I couldn't keep. If things didn't go to plan and somebody hated the day, I would feel responsible.

But Wembley wouldn't open discussions with me until Wrexham had confirmed their place in the final.

Kings and I had been to all the games during the cup run, which began with wins over Gloucester City, Folkestone Invicta and Boreham Wood at the Racecourse. We hadn't offered any travel for the

Quiet Zone members to away games before, but we'd kept the routine for home cup matches the same as every other fixture, even if not all the fans came. Cup matches are often very different at Wrexham because they cater to a completely different kind of clientele. Season ticket holders do get offered tickets first, but some don't take up the option in earlier rounds. The concourse isn't filled with the usual season ticket holders but tourists who have never been to the club before and have suddenly taken the chance. You can tell them apart because they're walking the concourses without a clue where anything is. It's a totally different ballgame. In that kind of atmosphere, the Quiet Zone is more important than ever.

The quarter-final trip to Notts County was when Kings and I really began to get invested in that cup run.

From his days working on *Dragonheart*, Kings would speak to lots of fans about their views on the competition and remembered the earlier rounds of the FA Trophy never being that well received among Wrexham fans – particularly after 2015, when Wrexham lost the final on penalties to North Ferriby United of the division below. North Ferriby don't even exist anymore because they ran up so much debt. Wrexham were winning the game quite comfortably until the manager Kevin Wilkin took off the captain Dean Keates and the team fell apart. Fans found it embarrassing and lots of fans started to disregard the 'Mickey Mouse' cup in which they ran the risk of losing to a lower-ranked team. The further Wrexham went in the 2021/22 season, though, the more the excitement built. How you feel about a competition becomes irrelevant once Wembley is on the horizon. A day out there becomes the priority.

We always had a good matchday experience at Notts County's Meadow Lane. Wheelchair users sit on the front row, which means we're exposed to the elements – many a time we've returned drowned rats – but right in front of our own fans, which is brilliant. The stand behind us is packed with Wrexham supporters, and our whole row was reserved for wheelchair users to give us twice the number of disabled seats we'd have at other grounds; wheelchair users don't have that experience everywhere.

However, one trip to Meadow Lane was especially memorable. My work at the club means that I have always been well known among our fanbase, even before *Welcome to Wrexham* aired. We alighted the accessible away travel bus to find swarms of police rounding up the rowdier Wrexham fans who had travelled on the train. Wrexham's hooligan firm is the 'Front Line', but its members look so young and baby-faced these days that some fans call them 'Nappy Liners'. Between the lines of police, we could see them, wired with adrenaline, all with their hoods up, faces obscured by snoods and scarves, dressed in Stone Island gear and CP Company jackets, trying to look big and clever. As each one went past us, they turned in our direction and said: 'Hiya, Kerry', 'Hiya, Kerry.' On and on they came, this conveyor belt of aspiring hooligans, with my passengers in stitches because I didn't know who any of these lads were but had, without realising, amassed all these new connections to Wrexham's Front Line.

That night in March 2022, Kings and I celebrated as Wrexham came from behind to win 2–1. The equaliser was scored by Dan Jarvis, and James Jones delivered the winner in the eighty-ninth minute, which was extra sweet for us because James was especially supportive of the role I did and would always go out of his way to have a conversation with me. All the nerves of the past forty-four minutes disappeared with the sudden realisation that County had virtually no time to reply. We went back to the minibus with the adrenaline still pumping, the fans singing late into the night.

We were one tantalising step away from Wembley. In our way, were Stockport, who were eleven points clear at the top of the National League. The rivalry had built with Stockport County in the second half of the season, as Wrexham gained momentum and started pushing for the National League title.

Ryan was visiting the club that evening and we bumped into him and one of his daughters before the match. They had arrived at 7 a.m. on a one-day return from New York and were both excited. 'Ryan,' I said, 'this could be massive for Wrexham.' I explained that I was thinking about running the Quiet Zone bus if we reached Wembley, and he knew that the Wembley trip, which would be televised, would be huge for what he and Rob were trying to build.

Not every fan, though, wanted him at the Racecourse. The superstitious lot didn't welcome him with open arms because Ryan's record watching Wrexham was so poor. Every time he came, we lost. It got to the point where fans would say: 'I hope he's not coming today!' At that point, his presence at matches was still a novelty – which shows how big this match was to Wrexham supporters.

In the ninetieth minute, the Wrexham striker Paul Mullin latched onto a long ball from Liam McAlinden and outpaced the approaching defenders to deftly chip the ball over the Stockport goalkeeper Ben Hinchcliffe with his first touch. He was alive outside the area four minutes later to read the flight of Christian Dibble's delivery and scoop up a misjudged header from Stockport's Liam Hogan. He lifted the ball over the keeper again before sprinting to the line to apply a final touch and make sure: 2–0. Wrexham were going to Wembley.

We think that this was the point where Ryan really fell in love with Wrexham and football – when it became far, far more than a business deal. When what was happening on the pitch, and the characters behind it all, eclipsed everything else. Fans spotted him at the ground and serenaded him: 'One Ryan Reynolds! There's only one Ryan Reynolds! One Ryan Reynolds!' Later, Ryan tweeted: 'I've never yelled this loud in my life. I thought I was going to die when he put the ball in the air like that.' He also used his social channels to describe it as a 'top ten life moment.' Those kinds of things – Ryan doing something small to make Wrexham so much bigger – have almost become the norm now, but they shouldn't have, because the whole thing is still absolutely ridiculous. Those pinch-me moments, where you're reminded of how global all of this has become, happen so often, and one part of your brain thinks: *Well, that's just Ryan – that's what he does.* Another part of you is still in disbelief that this is real life.

'Great! More work! More tickets to sell!' I joked with passing celebrating fans, but in reality, I was overcome with relief that we had made it. In the car park, I spotted Fleur climbing into her car.

'Am I OK to start sorting this – the Quiet Zone bus to Wembley?' I asked.

'Go for it, Kerry,' she smiled.

Wrexham had been to Wembley three times previously: twice in 2013 and once in 2015. Apart from the 2015 loss at North Ferriby, my last Wrexham match of that magnitude was the 2005 Football League Trophy Final at the Millennium Stadium in Cardiff, which Wrexham won 2–0 against Southend.

I was supposed to go for the 2013 FA Trophy Final vs Grimsby Town but I was hospitalised with a severe infection, confined to a room on my own while Kings went down with Dad, my brother Matt and Casey. Kings came to see me the night before the trip. As he talked of his travel plans, the snow started: driving snow that settled thickly and blanketed the streets. In the photos, Casey has not only her coat on but Kings's. He says it's the coldest he's ever been at a football match, even for someone who grew up in the house he did! Wrexham won that final 4–1 on penalties.

A few weeks later, Wrexham had what was then known as the Conference Premier Play-Off Final against Newport, losing 2–0 in the game most fans had prioritised and would have rather won. Kings says that Christian Jolley, who scored the first of Newport's two goals, had been a transfer target for Wrexham in January – talk about coming back to haunt us! Newport got promoted and Wrexham stayed in the National League.

Games like that were why Dad had vowed to never go to Wembley again. We knew he would – that's what football fans do. Wembley inspires such strong emotions in people because of the stakes. Dad was there for the 2015 game against North Ferriby. The abstinence never lasts long.

With Fleur's permission, I contacted Wembley to start discussing my plans in more detail. Fleur asked me to liaise with Wembley on Wrexham's behalf on everything: mascots, flag bearers and any information from the club linked to the trip.

I emailed a contact of Fleur's at Wembley and explained what we'd need for the Quiet Zone. How many rows would we be able to reserve? Could I have a section just for my families? Their initial response was that I couldn't book off one area for a big amount of people. I messaged back and explained what the Quiet Zone actually was and why it was so essential. I told them that I would be bringing people who had never been to an away game before and how they all wanted to be part of it. I impressed upon them the importance of getting this right. The key thing was that they were all together and had the comfort and familiarity of each other. I wanted my Quiet Zone stewards to sit in that block with them as well. Once they knew what I was after, Wembley worked with me.

The people in the Quiet Zone were used to a particular vantage point. Wembley sent back some pictures of the pitch from several different blocks and I picked the one that most resembled what they experienced at Wrexham. They were also used to sitting next to certain people. I planned that out, too.

Wembley sent across pictures of their sensory room as well. I needed it to be in a location that families could easily escape to if they needed it, which initially confused the FA customer engagement manager running it, Matthew Owen. 'We can't do that,' he said. 'It's only big enough for a certain number of families, and you'll need to tell us in advance which ones will need it on the day.'

'That isn't how we need it to work,' I explained. 'Children need to be able to come and go whenever they need to. We've got a bus of forty-eight people. How do I tell them that only three of them are allowed to go in the sensory room?'

He was brilliant once I'd laid out our reasoning, and said that we'd given him food for thought on how Wembley will run the sensory room in future because they had never considered that it would need to be used in that way. That was the week their sensory room opened, and we were the first club to use it. I hope the same man is still there because it's important that people running those kinds of facilities listen to and reflect the needs of the families they work with.

The Quiet Zone families' moods in the build-up to Wembley were really mixed. Some of them were bursting with excitement. Others were deeply anxious about the whole thing. I'd had to warn them that they wouldn't be treated like they are at Wrexham: there would be no waitress service, for example. In most cases, parents were more nervous than the kids themselves because some of these families had never done anything like this. One parent told me: 'I don't even know how he's going to cope travelling on a bus for all this time.' I took and made a lot of calls that week with people checking timings, what they could and couldn't take, how things would work, and what support I'd be providing.

But the whole point of the Quiet Zone bus was that anything went because all of the families were used to each other. They didn't have to mask or worry about what other people would think about them. They travelled with the stewards and we offered a sensory box with fidget spinners and ear defenders. I didn't want them on buses with general fans swearing, partying and getting lairy.

My wheelchair means that I can't travel on one of Pat's coaches, but I had another job: transporting Wrex, the Wrexham mascot.

'Kerry,' started Fleur during the week. 'I know it's not your job, but could you take Wrex to be cleaned?' It turned out that our van was the only one big enough to carry an anthropomorphic dragon. Kings and I duly drove the mascot to the dry cleaners on Wrexham Industrial Estate, and I picked him up the day before our big outing to Wembley.

At 7.30 a.m. on Sunday 22 May 2022, as the rising sun turned the skyline pink, we took pictures of Wrex in the passenger seat, gazing out the window and dreaming of a result. We posted the photos to social media and entertained ourselves on the trip down with the responses: 'Wrex is on his way! Wrex is coming with Kerry!'

En route, we received a call alerting us to a problem on the M40. We diverted to the M1 to find there had been another huge crash there. For two hours, we looked at the clock and could feel the time ebbing away. Wrex had to be delivered by 12.30 p.m. and we were already running late. We frantically texted the kitman Iwan, who was due to collect our precious cargo, and arranged to meet him an hour later outside one of the service doors at Wembley. We imagined the van's wheels screeching as Kings skidded round the corner like a heist scene in a film. By the time we arrived, a crowd of Wrexham fans had gathered in the doorway and lapped up Wrex's presence in the passenger seat.

Fleur and I had fought for the members of my powerchair football team to be flag bearers when the teams ran out on the pitch for kick-off. I think the competition had just assumed that the role would be taken by able-bodied kids, because that's what always happens, but we wanted it to be something really special. I had overseen the logistics, arranging for four wheelchair users to stay in a hotel the night before with their parents, who would chaperone them on the day.

Before announcing the news to the team, I'd called around the parents to make sure they were happy for their children to take part – the last thing I wanted was one kid in tears because his dreams had suddenly been dashed. I told the players at the training session the Friday before, and they were overjoyed. One teenager who had the opportunity, Harry, has since passed away. His parents said that seeing him be a flag bearer at Wembley was one of their best memories.

I wouldn't be with the team on the day, but I ran through their itinerary with them. They had to be at Wembley for a rehearsal at 8.30 a.m. and back by noon, so they had plenty of time to not only prepare but get excited for their big moment. I was their point of contact – I'd spoken to them all on our journey down to London and the night before – but my next stop was to meet Matthew Owen, with whom I'd discussed the sensory room. He took me through a glass-fronted corporate box with beanbags overlooking the pitch and into a separate room with a high-tech projector. You could plug in a particular setting – aquarium, say, or jungle – and it would project fish or foliage around the room. It didn't have as many toys as our sensory room in Wrexham, but the main thing was that the families could drop in as and when they needed to. Most clubs run their sensory rooms using a booking system, but that was never the way we'd worked at Wrexham. I smiled as I thought back to the email Fleur had sent me earlier that week: 'Only you, Kerry, would tell Wembley how to run their sensory room.'

I stopped by the area we'd set aside as the Wembley 'Quiet Zone' to check that the families were OK, and then I moved on to my seat. It was the same process we follow at Wrexham: I greet everybody on a matchday, check on the Quiet Zone before the fixture and then leave the stewards to it while I speak to the away fans. I go back at half time, and when the whistle goes for full time, I say goodbye to everybody and take queries and questions.

I was in tears watching the flag bearers, saying to Kings that I felt like a proud mother hen. They came to sit in the wheelchair spaces by us and showed me their matching T-shirts, explaining how they'd take them into school to show everybody the next day.

I don't switch off during matches. My dad always says that I might be a fan of Wrexham, but I never, ever watch the game. Things always crop up, some of them unforeseen issues, and I have to solve them. I've helped fans with medical issues, freed fans stuck in lifts. I'm so often the point of contact because I know everybody. I always see kick-off, but within thirty seconds, I'm gone. Every game, home or away, I'm fidgety, and I'm always on the phone, making sure I've not missed any calls or messaging: 'Is everything all right?' Wembley was no exception.

Given the problems on the road that Kings and I had encountered, one of those buses was late, pulling up ten minutes after kick-off. I put that responsibility on myself and felt guilty, even though I knew that it was nothing to do with me. There was a lot on my shoulders that day and I'd organised so much of that trip: the Quiet Zone, the sensory room access, the familiar face stewards, the flag bearers, the wheelchair users coming by bus.

My main memory of that day is anxiety. I know that stewards don't always check tickets at away games and fans like to just choose their own seats, so would everything in the Quiet Zone go without a hitch? I could see some stewards moving people from one seat to another and people trickling in after kick-off.

Up in the royal box, Ryan and Rob were under a different kind of pressure. Already the most-watched people in the stadium, they had invited the cameras from *Welcome to Wrexham* to share the moment with the world. The Wembley cameras had got there first, and the big screens continually cut to them. There was a shot of Ryan sipping his drinks. There was David Beckham, pottering about. A stoppage in play inevitably meant a shot of Beckham and Ryan talking.

This whole other subplot played out on the big screens at Wembley, and fans cheered whenever they came on the screen. Kit Harington, star of *Game of Thrones*, got a big reaction, as did *Anchorman*'s Will Ferrell. Also in their group was Ryan's wife Blake Lively. Fans waited to see who the next big name would be, and then their cheers would subside into muttering: 'I didn't realise he was here!' We joke now that this was the one time Ryan didn't call in on the Quiet Zone – because he always does.

Kings is probably similar to lots of fans in that he did feel that vicarious excitement and buzz despite being nowhere near them.

I'm very different in that I've never been overawed or starstruck by Ryan and Rob, which has probably served me well in my line of work, but it's funny to look back on moments like that one at Wembley because, again, all of it has become so normal for us now.

I always say that I feel sorry for whoever Wrexham are playing because they're overshadowed before they start. Maybe that's just me, because I'm a deep person who overanalyses everything. Perhaps those teams like life away from the spotlight. Certainly, that Wembley game introduced us all to the perils of it when, after Wrexham had gone 1–0 down to Michael Cheek's goal in the sixty-fourth minute, Wrexham substitute Jake Hyde headed home. The Wrexham end of Wembley exploded, as did Ryan and Rob – until the goal was ruled out for offside. To this day, Kings argues that the officials got that wrong and that the outcome would have been different had VAR been in play. In any case, Ryan and Rob had to endure days of coverage ridiculing them for not knowing the rules of football – even though all the fans celebrated, too. From that day, that was the one story the press picked to trump all the others. I found that really unfair.

Rob later told Jimmy Kimmel, the American chat show host, that David Beckham was the one to explain the offside rule to them, having been the only person in their box who understood the ref's decision: 'We were cheering, and we looked over at Beckham and he was just shaking his head.'

At full time, Ryan and Rob went down on the pitch to talk to the Bromley players, who were in disbelief at meeting them even as they partied with the trophy.

Wrexham did have a victory that day, however. It would have been better had they won on the pitch, but the success of the Quiet

Zone bus wasn't overshadowed by the defeat. Those fans just absolutely loved it. They'd been to Wembley, and they'd had the time of their lives. In the van, I cycled through messages from parents who didn't think their kids would have been able to cope with the experience – but the day had gone without a hitch.

As a parent of a Special Educational Needs child, going to Wembley with my son Joe for the game was a phenomenal experience.

It was our first away game and a daunting prospect – an experience I wasn't sure Joe could enjoy. With the Quiet Zone safeguarding in place, it was amazing for him and gave him the opportunity to enjoy the day. On the bus were the familiar faces from the Quiet Zone, from the friendly stewards who are always on hand to the families who have become friends to us. It created the same security we have at the Racecourse and gave Joe the consistency that was needed.

For Joe and others, this made the game accessible. It gave them a day and memories they will never forget.

This, and everything the Quiet Zone does, gives so many additional needs children and adults the chance to enjoy experiences that would otherwise be inaccessible.

Thank you for everything you do. Just seeing the enjoyment Joe got from being there is amazing.

– Karen

Millie was desperate to go to Wembley, as was I. Neither of us had ever been and it became apparent that the whole of Wrexham was going.

Our decision became much easier when you told us that you were arranging a Quiet Zone bus for the trip. Tickets were booked and Millie could be as excited as everyone else who was going. She had been desperate to go and now she could.

We dropped Millie and her Nan off for the bus in the morning. Our bus was in the front of the queue with Nicky standing outside. Millie recognised her immediately and got on the bus, no problem. It was full of adults and young people that saw in each other what was needed, supporting each other, chatting and just being there. My mum and Millie sat by a mum and her son: they spent the whole day together and they got each other. Sitting as a group in the stadium, supporting the team together, they had a fab day.

From never going on a bus and never going to an away game, this has helped Millie so much. We have made friends for life.

I replied to these messages and more as we set in for the long journey home – to the soundtrack of Dad resolving: 'I'm never going to Wembley again. I'm never going to Wembley again.'

That special day had such an impact on Harry's family that the headstone recently put on his grave has a picture of Harry on the pitch at Wembley. He has left behind such a huge imprint on my heart, which is why I wanted to include this piece of writing by his dad, Kevin Vaughan.

After receiving a phone call from Kerry to ask me if Harry would like to be a flag bearer against Bromley, I was unsure that he would want to do it.

How wrong was I?

He was beyond ecstatic about it. Harry couldn't believe that he had been picked to do such a thing along with the other three boys from powerchair football. He never, ever thought he would get to go on the pitch at Wembley, as opportunities like this just don't happen to children like Harry. On the day of the final, he was proud as punch to be representing Wrexham AFC through powerchair football. This gave him the opportunity to do what any child loved to do, and that was to play football with his mates.

We were met outside the ground on the day of the final by officials from Wrexham and the FA. After we went into the ground, we were met by other officials who went through what was going to happen during the day. They provided lunch for all the children, but Harry was far too excited to eat anything. We were led out onto the corner of the pitch to take in the atmosphere. Harry was so overwhelmed by it all. He couldn't actually believe he was at the side of the pitch he had only ever seen on TV.

We went back inside to get ready to be led out onto the pitch. In the corridor by the changing rooms, I explained to Harry where we were and the footballers that had walked through these corridors. As we went through the doors leading out to the pitch, we could hear the sound of the amazing crowd. Before the teams came out, I could see the excitement in Harry's face. It was the face of a child who couldn't actually believe he was here.

We were then led up to our seats, where his mum was waiting for us. The result unfortunately didn't go the way we wanted it to that day, but the only winner was Harry and the other boys. He felt so privileged to be given the opportunity by Kerry to bear the flag for Wrexham.

# CHAPTER FOURTEEN

# (TV) ROYALTY

After their first visit to Wrexham in October 2021, Ryan and Rob returned to America and their employment contract arrived in my inbox, as they'd promised. They went back to the US assuming that I would sign it instantly.

What they didn't see was my turmoil.

With my health issues – some of which have got worse over time – was I even capable of taking on this job? What about sick pay? What would happen if I was unable to work for the week? How long would I be able to work for?

In my days as a volunteer, I'd never had to worry about money. We'd never been well-off, but it didn't matter if I was ill for a week and unable to do anything for the club. My benefits paid me, and I didn't owe the club anything. If I went into paid employment and then couldn't go to work, how were we going to live? I would become the breadwinner of the family – but could I be relied upon? That weighed heavily on my shoulders. Within just a few months, I would go from doing a job I adored and loved purely because I adored and loved it to having to do it because I needed the wages. Would I lose my enjoyment of it?

'Why wouldn't you be up to it?' came the reply from everybody I confided in. 'You're already exceeding what they'd expect from you.' And they were right.

Realistically, I didn't ever not work for Wrexham, even on my worst days. When I was at my sickest, I would put a bucket at the side of my desk and vomit into it. In part that was because that's just who I am, but I was also the only person who knew how to do my job. But my point was that I *could* take a break if I had no other option. I had the freedom to step away without worrying about whether my role would still be there for me when I came back. I know there are protections in place for all employees, but we've all heard stories of people being driven out of workplaces when they can't keep up with the pace of the work or have too many absences. I have many hospital appointments every year.

It might sound like I had no aspirations, but receiving benefits meant that I had the comfort of knowing that the money would always come in no matter what happened to me. I'm not sure those worries ever go away when you have a disability or chronic illness, even though I've more than earned my stripes at Wrexham. If I ever have to leave due to ill health, we'll have to start the process of signing up for benefits again – and the system has changed so much already that I'm not sure what I'd receive.

People couldn't always understand those anxieties because they saw someone who had proven themselves more than capable of performing the role. They thought that I'd jump at the offer, but I just wasn't ready to sign.

'You're doing the job already,' Fleur would say in our numerous conversations on the subject. She understood my anxieties but kept emphasising that this was simply recognition of the job I'd been doing for years.

'Surely, there's going to be more commitment if there's money involved,' I protested.

'You can't do any more than you're doing,' Fleur answered. 'They just want to pay you for your commitment.'

Several times, Kings and I sat with a pen and paper and drew up a list of positives and negatives, but it never seemed to help me come up with an answer. In the end, the decision came down to one simple fact: I didn't want to leave. In so many walks of life, people had treated me differently and made me feel like I was invisible – but never at Wrexham. There, I'm just Kerry. That means so much to me. Volunteers were going. If I didn't take the job, would they hire someone else? What would that mean for me? It was time to take a leap of faith.

I didn't sign on the dotted line until 1 March 2022.

• • •

The wait for *Welcome to Wrexham* to air felt interminable. I dreaded seeing the final cut – not because I was unhappy with what I'd said, but because I didn't know how the film crew would stitch it together. As much as the crew had the ability to make me look good, they could show me up if things didn't come across well. I had no control over how people would perceive me. Every full-time staff member was invited to the Centenary Club to watch the first two episodes, which came out in August. The mood was guarded, and everyone remained that way until they saw their own episode.

The first two episodes focused mainly on Ryan and Rob's purchase of the club and the town's history. Rob was shown as the driving force behind the project, having become eager to purchase a football club after watching the Netflix documentary *Sunderland*

'*Til I Die* and enlisting Ryan's help because he needed someone with Hollywood money and star power. The real star of the show, though, was Wayne Jones, the owner of The Turf – the go-to meeting place for fans before matches and the oldest public house at any sports stadium in the world.

Wayne became a staple of the series and now welcomes customers from all over the world who visit Wrexham and drop into the pub. Apparently, lots of overseas viewers thought that The Turf was just a TV set! Wayne is a top guy, and these days we wind each other up about which one of us is more famous (I think he's *way* more famous than me, but he's so unaffected by all of it). On the invitations for my fiftieth birthday party I wrote that everybody had to come to the 'world famous' Turf. When Rob and Ryan visit, it's not unheard of for them to just wander in, and fans – especially the Americans – are always thrilled at the thought of drinking with them. Wayne is dealing with upmarket clientele these days.

Episode one, entitled 'Dream', showed us the Zoom call with the WST from the other side before the next episode, 'Reality', showed the scale of the challenge that Ryan and Rob, still cut adrift on the other side of the world at this point in the show, had taken on. It recorded the team missing out on the play-offs and finishing in eighth place, extending our stay in the National League to a fourteenth year. Kings and I featured briefly on footage we'd captured on my phone, giving our reaction to the team's form – watching it, I was absolutely dying of embarrassment!

'Look at you on the telly!' everyone gushed. I was mortified, and I'd only been on there for a few seconds.

But I did love watching the show when I was safe from seeing myself. The best bit was seeing things behind the scenes that I didn't know had happened, even if it was surreal watching people I worked with on the big screen.

I know the Racecourse like the back of my hand – I've been in the changing room thousands of times – but watching it all rendered through such high production values on television was bizarre. I think that we've been very, very lucky. Every club would love to have that level of exposure, fans would love to have that level of insight and everyone involved would love to have treasured memories documented like that. We have the Ryan and Rob era recorded for posterity, which is a real privilege.

The biggest shock of all – and the thing people were most eager to ask me about once the show aired – was seeing Phil Parkinson in the dressing room. I've met him hundreds of times and I know him as the most pleasant, placid, well-mannered and well-spoken man. When he sees me, he always makes an effort to chat, even to the point of discussing volunteering opportunities: he had told his wife about me, and she was thinking of finding voluntary work somewhere.

Another time, I couldn't work the ramp on my van while I was at the club on my own. 'Kerry!' he said when he saw me struggling. 'Can I help? What do I need to do?' He's the manager, and he got down on his hands and knees to fix my ramp.

Then we cut to the dressing room and it's all effing, blinding and screaming his head off. Who is he?! It's unbelievable; I've never met that guy. Talk about chalk and cheese. Though far removed from the Phil Parkinson I know, the film crew – who tracked his expletives with a 'Phil's enthusiasm' counter in the corner of the screen – clearly relished it and thought it made for great TV.

The end of the second episode included a preview of what was to come: Rob pacing up and down outside his trailer on a studio lot as he tried to persuade Phil to come and work for Wrexham. Phil hadn't wanted his side of the conversation to be recorded so the filming had been done from a distance. As it happened, he was sat behind me in the Centenary Club and it resulted in the bizarre situation of me watching Phil studying himself. The film crew had caught the moment Rob came off the call, unsure whether he had been able to win over a cautious and sceptical Phil. I turned around to admonish him: 'At least I'd speak to poor Rob!'

At home, we watched these scenes play out in full in episode three, including, of course, a happy resolution when Phil finally agreed to come on board and started assembling his coaching and playing staff.

Then I appeared on the screen.

I was always very nervous and apprehensive when *Welcome to Wrexham* aired, aware that I could pop up at any moment. Then, suddenly, there I was, watching Kings help past Kerry get ready for the game. I watched myself discuss my phone call with Rob, what my role involved and what happened during my working week. Then came voiceovers from Ryan and Rob.

'We thought it was important to hire somebody who was going to create accountability in terms of the stadium being accessible,' Ryan said.

'She exemplifies the spirit of the town,' continued Rob. 'So many people who worked at the club were volunteers, and Kerry was one of those people. She was doing the exact job we had hired her to do, and had been for many years, for free.'

The scene cut to me explaining that I was preparing to move into full-time employment and that the decision to do so had brought with it great anxiety. I felt a wave of relief as I watched, and I knew then that I could trust the editing team. I was delighted with how I came across. When I later learned that Rob, with whom I've always treasured my relationship, is part of the production team, I knew that I shouldn't have fretted as much as I did.

There had been an initial boom of attention when Ryan and Rob took over, but the release of *Welcome to Wrexham* took it to another level again. For the first time, viewers around the globe were taken inside the club and guided by Ryan and Rob as they met a new cast of characters. We might not be top of the Premier League, but Ryan and Rob's involvement has made us one of the most famous football clubs in the world outside of the big leagues.

On the eve of the show's premiere, I posted to Facebook: 'I can't quite believe in twenty-four hours that little old Wrexham will be known worldwide. How mad is that?' Yet I don't think anybody, myself included, realised how big an impact the show was going to have. I would receive messages from Wrexham fans posing beneath billboards in LA and all over the world, but those billboards alone don't come close to capturing the impact the show had on its audience. Instantly, emails started to arrive from people all around the world – slowly, first, and then in droves.

People told me they'd begun following Wrexham solely because of my work at the club. I had a family who flew over because they were so besotted with the work I'd done for families with disabilities. They asked to meet me, and while we talked I video-called their disabled son back in Australia who had been unable to make the journey. Who flies all that way because it would mean so much for their son to speak to *me* via video? Another couple flew in from America for one of the games, but also wanted to meet me and asked if they could attend a powerchair football session. What an honour to have people asking to meet me and see my work.

People wrote that I had changed their lives, even though they had never been anywhere near Wrexham. They had spoken to their own football and soccer clubs to tell them of the things I'd implemented, and clubs around the world started to follow suit as they messaged me to ask for my thoughts on how they could make their facilities more inclusive. One person's letter really touched me.

Dear Kerry,

I just wanted to take a moment to personally reach out and say thank you. I've had the privilege of seeing how small acts of thoughtfulness can create life-changing moments for individuals and families. Seeing what you've helped bring to life at Wrexham AFC is nothing short of inspiring. Your exact words – 'Even the smallest of changes make a huge impact on people that you're trying to help' – captures the truth that so many miss. But you haven't just said those words; you've lived them. And the impact shows. You've created an environment where fans of all abilities feel not just welcomed but valued. You've turned Wrexham into a place where everyone can belong, celebrate and be part of something bigger and special. It's hard to put into words how powerful this is.

Your work is not only changing lives; it's setting a gold standard for what inclusion in sport looks like. My hope is that other clubs take notice of you and follow your lead, because the world needs more Kerrys. Thank you for your heart, your dedication, and for showing us all what's possible when empathy and action come together.

I have a folder called 'positive emails' where I save messages like this. Sometimes I find it all puzzling: why does a stranger feel so compelled to write that to me? We've never met. It's hard to wrap your head around the fact that people have taken their time to put pen to paper (or fingers to keyboard) to contact you with something so meaningful and heartfelt, especially when I feel like I'm just doing my job. I didn't set out to have that kind of global impact; all I wanted to do was try and make a difference and make people feel welcome. But Kings says that's why people responded to me, because they could see that I was genuine. I can't put into words what receiving messages like that means.

By the end of the first series, it felt like everywhere I went, somebody recognised me. That included a holiday in London, when a man walked towards me and went: 'I thought it was you! Wait until my girlfriend knows I've met you – we love *Welcome to Wrexham*. You're amazing at the work you do.' Often, I'm referred to as 'Kerry off *Welcome to Wrexham*' or, around the town, 'Kerry off the telly'. On a cruise, one person walked towards me with a picture of me on their phone and the words: 'We love the show!' Another family rushed over to me on a different cruise holiday and said: 'We knew it was you, right on the first day when we left Southampton!' People ask for pictures, and I'm not quite sure what to say. Meekly, I just thank them for their kind words.

I'm little old Kerry from Wrexham doing a job I love. Full stop. That is the end of it. I might now be good at that job – but I'm the same person I always was. I always insist that it's the role, not me, that makes the difference, but it's true that you need the right person to make a job like mine what it is.

I would absolutely not put myself on Ryan and Rob's level of fame, but, bizarrely, Rob and I ended up having a conversation about the perils of celebrity on one of his next visits to the club. Rob had been browsing the club shop when word got out that he was there, and fans began to swarm at the windows for a glimpse of him. He slipped out through the back door and into the offices where I was working. Rob leaned up against the wall chatting to me about my job, what I was up to and how everything was going.

'You've had a taster of what it's like to be us,' he said, when I brought up *Welcome to Wrexham*. 'What's it like to be famous, Kerry?'

'It's absolutely mad,' I said, only half joking. 'It's getting ridiculous. I get recognised everywhere I go. It's crazy. I feel like I need to do myself up to go out to the shops just in case people ask for a picture. I'd hate to be you or Ryan, with all you have to put up with.'

Rob found this very amusing. 'Welcome to our world,' he grinned.

He was also looking for characters and plotlines for series two, and I mentioned the Quiet Zone. It had such a profound, transformative impact on so many families, and Rob was interested in covering it – which was how he found Millie Tipping, who is the focus of the episode 'The Quiet Zone' in series two.

I feel such a responsibility when talking about the Quiet Zone in the media because the families who need that service are so vulnerable. Everybody at Wrexham would tell you the same: the Quiet Zone is my baby. I take full responsibility for it, and you really feel the weight of that responsibility when, on a regular basis, families tell you that they physically could not come to games without that area.

I don't take that lightly. I don't want families upset, and I want their experience to run as smoothly as possible. I do lots of talking with staff around key fixtures to make sure that we can provide the best service. I'm incredibly proud of what we've created. It's a balance of wanting to show off that work to inspire other football clubs to follow suit while also being mindful of the needs of the families when involving them in this kind of production.

Paul Mullin and his son Albi, who has nonverbal autism, also featured in that same episode, which would become one of the most acclaimed of the series. While sharing his family story, Paul and Millie formed a lovely bond, and they now often chat to each other before games. Paul knew everything the club had in place to support autistic supporters even before he joined, and he's since been a brilliant advocate for the work I do.

'If you need anything at all – if you need my backing – just let me know,' he's always said, and he's been as good as his word. There have been times when I've felt children in the Quiet Zone have needed a pick-me-up and I've mentioned this to Paul, who will go out of his way to help, meeting them before games or in his lunch hour during the week.

Ben Tozer has left now, but he was always amazing with the kids as well. To be fair, most of the players are. Millie stands in the same spot outside the players' entrance before every game and will tell each of them that they're going to score.

I saw her recently giving striker Steven Fletcher strict instructions: 'When you score, come to our Quiet Zone corner,' she said. 'Don't go to the other corner.'

'I remember, Millie,' he laughed. 'I know what I've got to do.'

She said the same to Jack Marriott. 'We'll see you later,' he promised.

Wrexham winger James McClean learned that he was autistic as an adult, and he was also familiar with our work before he came to the club. He has always spoken highly of Wrexham's accessibility efforts and spoke publicly about his condition to show his daughter

Willow-Ivy, who is also autistic, that he understands her. He told me that he had seen on the show the impact of the Quiet Zone and that he was keen to support us.

Even without Ryan, Rob, Paul and James, people were really interested in the Quiet Zone because of what it represented: sadly, spaces like it are still very rare in football. Those four putting their voices behind it increased that interest tenfold and has meant that a lot more people respect the purpose of that area. Previously, we received complaints from fans who didn't understand why there were empty seats in that stand when the rest of the ground was full, but they get it now.

The first series of *Welcome to Wrexham* didn't get its Hollywood ending, as the club missed out on promotion to League Two after losing in the semi-finals of the play-offs to Grimsby.

I don't think anybody really expected Wrexham to win promotion that 2021/22 season because everything was still so new. Stockport were flying ahead; only around Christmas did Wrexham begin to find form. That charge to the summit seemed to happen so quickly, but it was the 3–0 win over Stockport in front of 10,000 people at the Racecourse, which temporarily put us top of the league on goal difference, that really made us think we could do it one day. Kings and I travelled to Wrexham's final game of the season knowing that Stockport needed to lose against Halifax Town, but they went 1–0 up after ten minutes and 2–0 up before the hour.

Wrexham lost their own game 3–0 to Dagenham and Redbridge. It would be the play-offs.

For the last twenty-five minutes of that game against Dagenham, though, our travelling fanbase sang ceaselessly. It gave me chills. I took my phone from my pocket and recorded them because I had never heard anything like that. Even after full time, as the fans piled out of the stadium single file, they continued to sing: 'Olé, olé, olé, Oh… Wrexham FC! We're the Red Army!'

It was spine-tingling to hear. *Listen*, they seemed to say to the players, *we will back you all the way in the play-offs*. It was another sign of the special bond that was building.

We lost 5–4 to Grimsby in the play-offs after extra time. Kings was an emotional mess in the stands, muttering away: 'I don't want to play Dorking Wanderers any more.' We resigned ourselves to another season in the National League, but we were beyond fed up with it by then.

Sadly, Nan passed before she ever got to see *Welcome to Wrexham*.

After Granddad's death, my relationship with her had grown even stronger. Barely a day would pass when we didn't chat, with her always finishing the call by 7 p.m. in time for her beloved *Emmerdale*.

She fell at Kings's fortieth birthday party and ended up in an ambulance, after which Kings used to joke that she mustn't spoil his next big birthday. On his fiftieth, she wished him a happy birthday, even though she was so poorly. Then, in true Nan style, she had the last laugh, as she passed away later that day.

In her final years, she wrote a letter to me, with the instructions that I only read it at home: she said how much she treasured our special relationship and thanked me for the constant calls. I couldn't ever see a life without her.

At her funeral, I read a poem. I simply didn't know how I'd hold it together, but I knew I couldn't let Nan down. That was the very last thing I could do for her.

• • •

There had been rumours for weeks that King Charles and Queen

Camilla would be coming to Wrexham to celebrate our new city status, granted in December 2022 as part of the civic honours to mark Queen Elizabeth II's Platinum Jubilee. Everyone we knew was convinced that royalty would visit.

The club, though, said nothing. Not one word. Amid that silence, the buzz intensified. Still, there was no word from the club, and no sign that Friday 9 December would be anything other than business as usual.

At 8.30 p.m. on Thursday, my phone rang: Fleur Robinson.

'You might have heard the rumours,' Fleur began. 'Well, tomorrow, King Charles and Queen Camilla are coming.'

'Right.'

'You're personally going to be meeting them.'

'Right.'

'I need you to get four or five players in their powerchairs and lined up ready to greet them both in the 1864 Suite. They're going to come through the players' entrance, see the changing rooms, come down the tunnel and out onto the pitch to meet all the players, the manager and the top staff. Then they'll move across to the Macron stand to talk to the rest of the staff. After that they'll come up the stairs to the 1864 Suite, and you need to be the first person that they see as they come through the door to speak to the powerchair football players.'

Fleur ran through etiquette and protocol and what I had to remember. 'Get everybody in place, then don't move,' she said. 'Don't leave the room. And it's ma'am like jam. Not *ma-a-a-am*, and not *mom*. You mustn't put your hand out; you have to wait until they put their hand out to you. Don't speak to them until they've addressed you.

'And one last thing – you can't tell any of the team why they're there,' she said.

'How will I get them there if I don't tell them anything?' I responded.

'No!' Fleur insisted. 'You mustn't tell.'

I spent the next hour ringing around the players. 'You will want to be there,' I said, as they pressed me for details. 'Can you just trust me on this? Can you be there tomorrow morning?'

One lad lived all the way in Pwllheli, almost two hours from Wrexham – and I wasn't able to tell him any more than that. All I could say was that it would be worth it; that it was something really, really special.

I am a mega royalist. I always have been, ever since the world was introduced to Princess Diana. I've dragged Kings around all the palaces and houses apart from Balmoral. We went to Buckingham Palace for my fortieth birthday, with Mum, Dad and Casey in the back, and booked parking in the palace in one of the blue badge spaces.

'We've booked in,' we said to the palace guards as we pulled up.

'That's absolutely fine,' they said, 'but we've got a royal on their way. Can you drive down the Mall?' On our way down, we saw police cars and a car with blacked-out windows coming the other way. As we pulled towards the gate, armed police with guns leapt into action and ducked down to look under our van.

'They're not real!' Casey snorted.

'Yes, Casey,' I said. 'They are.'

'As if!' she scoffed, unimpressed.

From inside our van, we could hear the clicks of camera flashes and the excited tones of tourists. 'Who's this? Who's in that van?'

Because I was a wheelchair user, I was able to use Queen Elizabeth II's golden lift. We did the whole tour, including the royal stables. We were initially disappointed that we couldn't get into the Buckingham Palace Garden because the public access route isn't wheelchair-accessible, but we got lucky with a really friendly staff member, who guided us there via the Queen's own private gateway and garden!

On the Friday of Wrexham's royal visit, I organised the powerchair football players in the way Fleur had requested and the moment had come to tell them why they were all gathered there. They looked at each other in disbelief and were as excited as I was.

Try as I might, I couldn't follow Fleur's briefing to the letter. I couldn't just sit still, waiting for the King and Queen to materialise. I had to know what was going on.

'Am I allowed to move?' I said to someone from our media team.

'Well, you can – but everybody else had better stay here,' he said, pointing to the line of players. 'And you'd better get back here quickly.'

I took the lift up to level two and went along to the original wheelchair viewing platform. From there, I watched as the King and Queen came down the tunnel and shook hands with the players and staff from the men's and women's teams. They spoke to Ryan, Rob and Shaun Harvey, with Fleur making the introductions before the royal couple asked questions about everyone's role at the club. Queen Camilla was familiar with the Wrexham journey and told one of the players that it was 'an extraordinary story'.

As King Charles moved along the Macron stand, I could see the staff sitting up straighter and elbowing each other. I read their lips: 'He's about to walk past us!' I headed back to the lift to get in my spot just as the King approached the building with Camilla.

As they spoke with me, I could see Ryan and Rob craning their necks like two naughty schoolboys, eager to hear what we all said. Fleur introduced me and explained how I'd been at the club initially as a volunteer before taking on my role full-time. She added that we were the first powerchair football club in Wales.

'Congratulations on your role,' the King said. 'It sounds like you do a wonderful job.'

He asked questions about the sport: how it worked, why the chairs had bumpers. He moved along the line, at which point Camilla started to speak to me. She was really chatty and friendly, and we talked in detail about what being Wrexham's disability liaison officer involved.

'You support all those people?' she said in disbelief. 'This is wonderful.'

Charles later praised the football club when he spoke to dignitaries, saying that it was 'busy putting Wrexham on the map as never before.'

*Welcome to Wrexham*, of course, captured part of the visit none of us had seen: Ryan and Rob going to what Ryan described as 'monarchy boot camp,' or what you and I would call lessons with an etiquette coach. You can see now why cameras have never really left: every day, there is a new chapter of the story to film.

'I never thought we'd have royalty at the club,' I told the press after the visit of the King and Queen. 'Now, we've had Hollywood royalty and real royalty!'

# CHAPTER FIFTEEN

# 'YOU INSPIRE ME'

### APRIL 2023

In a clip that would be used for *Welcome to Wrexham* and repeated on news clips and social media compilations, a cameraman had caught me breaking down in tears at the end of the match against Boreham Wood which qualified us for automatic promotion to League Two at the end of the 2022/23 season. I was simply so, so overwhelmed with emotion and joy at finally escaping the National League after all this time. They had done it, finally. As we left the grounds, I reflected on how long the journey had been. I was so proud – of our club, of how far we had come, of all of the adventures we'd had and the sunny days that awaited. I breathed deeply, as though I'd just come up for air, taking in that particular kind of euphoria and joy that only football can give.

The 1864 Suite houses, in theory, about eighty-five people. On the night of our promotion-securing win it hosted many more.

The plan had been for the players' celebrations to take place in the Centenary Club, and only full-time members of staff had been invited to join them. The Cent, however, was still full of fans who wanted to carry on partying with the players. Then we got word: 'Staff, move out. Don't make a scene. Don't say anything to anybody. Just start leaving and making your way over.'

Most staff made their way across the pitch. I can't. I went outside, around the car park and the club shop and into the lift in the 1864 Suite's guest entrance still with my cider in hand. As the lift doors opened, I made out the shifting forms of players and their partners dancing on tables to the beats of each of their football chants.

Kings and I sat by the door and surveyed the scene. Players embraced us, their medals dangling in front of our faces as they bent to talk to us. We had grown to know them and their families, and that evening, we were all colleagues celebrating their extraordinary success at the fifteenth time of asking. To win the National League after that long felt cathartic, and people were ready to let out lots of emotions from the wild ride to promotion, which tipped into the kind of joy Wrexham had not seen for generations.

By this point, the players were used to Ryan and Rob, who were often in the changing room or filming skits with them. 'Come in!' came the shouts from the room as Ryan and Rob appeared at the threshold. 'Enjoy the party!' A bizarre aspect of Ryan and Rob's existence is that this – a historic promotion party at which the players who had just become legends were about to get drunk out of their minds – is one of the places where they're most likely to be treated normally. Following shortly behind the pair was Humphrey, who appeared with the trophy – which quickly disappeared into the middle of the room after we'd had a photo with it.

Rob folded me into a hug and kissed my cheek. He crouched down, and we started to talk.

'I can't believe we've got out of the National League so quickly,'

I said to him. 'This means so much. I've said it before, but I owe everything to Wrexham. I just had so little confidence before I came here. This job changed my life. I found myself again.'

'We couldn't have done it without you, Kerry.'

'I think you could.'

'I'm serious. You're as important as every player in this room. You're just as important to us. We *couldn't* have done this without you.'

I talked a little more about the impact coming to work at Wrexham had on my life when I was, without realising it, at my lowest. For so long, I, like so many others, had lived a half-life: my house was my whole world, social media was like looking through people's windows, watching events unfold that I believed I could never be part of, and I struggled with loneliness. I was cut off from society, without community and a wider purpose, with no idea how to change it and, if I'm honest, no belief that I ever would. I made the best of the things and people that brought me joy and meaning – Kings and Casey, of course – but had resigned myself to thinking that way of life would be my forever.

Going to Wrexham had changed all that, and, in a beautiful circle, I was now helping other people expand their horizons through my work at the same football club that had helped me. I wanted to show people that there could be more – that so much life was waiting for them. My story had proven that we all have more to offer than we realise.

'All I want to do is just inspire one person,' I said, explaining this to Rob.

'You inspire people every day of the week, Kerry,' he replied. 'You inspire hundreds of people. You inspire me. My life is richer for having you in it.'

In the background, Paul Mullin's song rang out: 'We've got Mullin! Super Paul Mullin!' The room seemed to quiver and vibrate with movement. There was a free-for-all at the bar, which was in the process of being drunk dry so quickly – no one had planned to be in this bar – that the bar staff would soon run out of spirits. My intimate conversation with Ryan had taken place in the presence of boom mics and cameras; this time, Rob and I were the room's sole moment of stillness as tables quaked beneath the weight of dancing players and hands clapped and feet stomped.

That was the first time I'd ever had that kind of personal moment with Rob. Since our first call, he'd often asked for my opinion on club matters – what I thought of all the changes and how the staff felt – probably because I'd been with him on his Wrexham journey from the beginning, but I was so touched by his sincerity in the midst of such a big moment for the club and his ownership.

Rob's words that night are part of the reason you are reading this book now.

I can't quite understand where the interest in me – little old Kerry from Wrexham – comes from. I'm not sure I ever will understand until the day I leave the club. But that interest is there, and it's thanks to the platform Ryan and Rob gave me the minute they purchased the club and shared their footage with the world. Maybe them coming into my orbit, and the experiences we've shared, had a bigger purpose. How does someone like me, with all I've survived, get to experience something like this? And what could my story mean to somebody feeling as lost as I once was?

*If she can do it, maybe I can.*

With the barrels empty, some players departed to town – only to find that they were mobbed wherever they went. Kings and I saw footage later of one fan driving his car with his boot thrown open and a Wrexham player sat there, waving.

Some made their way back quite quickly to a now-deserted Centenary Club to carry on partying. Not many went home. Some slept on the physio's treatment tables and others in their cars. Kings and I arrived at the club the next morning to find a few players only just going home.

'I'm so glad you're here,' one of them said to a member of the media team who'd arrived at the same time as Kings and me. 'You can open the gate so I can go to the loo.' He'd slept in his car.

A few days later I contacted Julie to see where the staff were congregating together to watch the players' bus parade.

'You're riding on a bus,' she said. That was beyond my wildest dreams.

• • •

I arrived at the Racecourse and looked up to see three red double-decker buses, each decorated with gold lettering. One was for the women's team to mark their promotion. One was for the men's team, bearing words like 'Champions' and 'Going to the EFL'. The third was the staff bus.

Or it should have been. Only one bus had a ramp: the players'. We had to swap buses – all because of me.

That wasn't the only thing that didn't go to plan. Fleur had scheduled forty minutes for our journey from the Racecourse to the town centre and back. Then 40,000 people turned up.

We watched dots of red move beneath us like ants as the bus failed to manage even a crawl past The Turf. It just couldn't move, hemmed in by the mass of people who had come out to celebrate. We saw fans climb lampposts and traffic lights, watched them waving from the tops of buildings with flags and flares as others hammered on the windscreen and pressed their cameras against the windows to get pictures.

When the buses eventually pulled past Ysgol Plas Coch, I picked out my mum and dad in the crowd. I saw their faces crumple with emotion, and I broke down, too: I was so proud that I had given them the opportunity to see me be a part of that parade. Spotting Spencer Harris and his wife outside Saith Seren was the hardest. From a street corner, they blew kisses to us. I wished he could have been on the bus with us and seen what we were able to see. It would have been so deserved.

Four and a half hours later, we arrived back at the Racecourse. Security rushed to close the gates because a conga line of fans had followed the bus. We all alighted and dispersed quickly, seeking the nearest toilet and a bite to eat. The security manager on our bus said he had worked on a celebration parade for a Premier League team and the atmosphere hadn't been anything like this – and I believe him.

Ben Foster had been followed by a rumour that he would be leaving the club that summer, but there was a twinkle in his eye as he kissed me on the cheek.

'If that doesn't make you want to stay, I don't know what will,' I smiled.

'That was awesome,' he said definitively. 'I'll be staying.'

Parkinson walked past us in a daze, utterly gobsmacked. The players were physically and mentally exhausted having been on the bus for so long – in that time we could have got to London with almost an hour to spare.

'Forty minutes, you said!' I shouted across to Fleur.

'I only gave it half an hour originally,' Fleur said. 'I upped it to forty minutes.'

• • •

Wrexham's first game in League Two took place against Milton Keynes Dons FC on 5 August 2023 – my birthday.

I posted to Facebook: 'Looking forward to sharing my birthday with 10,000 friends.' The newly renamed Cae Ras (Racecourse) would be heaving for Wrexham's first game back in the league.

I would also be sharing the day with somebody else: Ryan, who was arriving unexpectedly. The minute we learned he was coming we needed to prepare down at the Quiet Zone. He visits us every time and, when he turns up, fans from other stands will try to infiltrate the area. His security help our stewards to make a makeshift barrier protecting our families, who, of course, come into the area because it's calmer than other stands.

We got word that Ryan had been in The Turf, meaning he would be stopping by on the way to his box. As he came around the corner, someone else was with him: Hugh Jackman.

Ryan enveloped me in a hug. 'How are you, Kerry?' he began, before turning to Hugh. 'This is Kerry,' he said. 'She takes care of our Quiet Zone. In fact, if it wasn't for her, there wouldn't *be* a Quiet Zone.' He turned back to me. 'Tell Hugh all about what it represents and why you've done it.'

One thing I like about Ryan is that he always introduces me to whoever he's with, and very much gives credit to his staff – more than I'm due, I feel sometimes – and allows us to explain for ourselves the work we've done. It was the same when Channing Tatum came to shoot the Super Bowl advert in February 2025. Channing didn't come to the Quiet Zone himself, but we bumped into him as he came down the stairs to go to the players' changing rooms.

I talked Hugh through the history of the Quiet Zone: how I'd set it up, and how it was for fans who simply wouldn't be able to come to the stadium without the things we had put in place. I explained about our stewards, their relationships with the families, the sensory room behind the seats that had started life as a disused storeroom.

'This is phenomenal,' Hugh exclaimed. 'What you've created here is so special. You should be so proud. I'm so proud of you.'

As talk turned to the game and the sell-out crowd – my 10,000 friends – I mentioned it was my birthday.

'I'm just so impressed,' Hugh said before he left. 'Come here and give me a hug. Happy birthday.'

I texted Joanne: 'Guess who I've just had a kiss from.'

'Your life gets weirder and weirder by the week,' came her reply.

This is just how things at the club have gone since the takeover. I never, ever thought I'd meet Ryan Reynolds. Then you do. Then you meet the King and Queen. Then Hugh Jackman walks out and gives you a birthday kiss. I still think, *what's next?* I've also had the pleasure of meeting Ryan's wife Blake and Rob's wife Kaitlin Olson, along with most of the cast of *Always Sunny*. Charlie Day – who writes, stars in and produces the show with Rob – said: 'I know you! I've watched you off the telly!'

'You're the most beautiful soul, inside and out,' Kaitlin said to me that same day. 'I don't think you realise just how famous you are in America.'

I wonder sometimes if that's just what Americans are like: all positive politeness and exaggeration. By comparison, my reply was a little more realistic. 'I'll never know how famous I am there because

I can't fly to America,' I said, explaining about the pressure in my head since the cerebral bleed.

Before the MK Dons game, the club contacted me with news of Rob's idea. He wanted to sit in the Quiet Zone and experience it himself so that he could understand what it was. He asked for ear defenders, and, on the day, the weather was so miserable that he also wore one of our red ponchos.

'Make sure you go and speak to him, like you do everyone else,' I said to my stewards. 'See how he's doing.'

Before Rob's arrival, I briefed my families. 'Do not make a beeline for him. Do not keep getting up to go to him. Stay in your seats. Watch the game. Let him have this experience.' That was the first time Rob had been there, and he gave us good feedback.

Ryan is a frequent visitor to the Quiet Zone, but he can't stay for the whole match because nobody, in any of the stands, would stay in their seat. He visits with the best of intentions, making such a fuss and going above and beyond for the families. He once came with twenty Wrexham baseball caps, which he signed and handed out to each of the children. We have to be very careful about his visits and manage them properly. Although he's trying to do something so lovely, some of the kids who are less confident and don't put themselves forward don't get as much time with him, which can upset them. I explained this to Ryan, who hadn't realised that was happening. Now, he is mindful and will go up to the steps and talk to the quieter ones at the back.

We have to think about striking a balance, too. I want to give the kids in the Quiet Zone a completely normal experience, and sometimes that means that we don't want them to be singled out for special treatment. Ryan is aware of that and will now sometimes talk to kids on the front row from outside the Quiet Zone. I am glad that Ryan has been willing to listen and work with us on that. All he wants to do is the right thing.

It's another reminder of how bizarre life has become when part of your job role is making sure people get equal time with Ryan Reynolds.

• • •

Earlier that year, on 24 January 2023, someone even more exciting had entered my life: my granddaughter Hali.

Everyone's child, of course, is the most important one in the world – but there was something about Casey, and the fact that we never expected to have her, never expected her to survive, that makes that bond so intense. She is so well loved. Her telling us that she was expecting made for one of the best days of our lives.

I was working at the club when Casey went into a labour lasting more than forty hours. During that time, whenever I came through the entrance at the club shop to get to the office, I would shake my head at their expectant faces. 'No,' I'd shrug. 'Still hasn't had her.'

'Are you going to go?' one staff member said at closing time. 'There's no way I'd go home without calling in – not after this long.'

'There's no way they'll let me in,' I said to Kings, 'but we need to try.'

Kings stayed outside as I went to the hospital desk. It was the news I'd expected: that Casey was in the delivery suite and I wouldn't be allowed in. 'Can you just let me know if she's doing OK?' I asked. 'Can you tell her that her mum's here? Can I at least give her a hug?'

Then Casey's partner Rhys appeared, gesturing at me to follow him.

'You time things right!' Casey grimaced as we entered. 'I want you to stay.'

'No,' I said. 'This is special to you and Rhys. I just wanted to check on you. How exciting that you're about to have her!'

'Stay,' Casey insisted. It wasn't that she hadn't wanted me there, but that she'd never, ever considered that she would be allowed more than one birthing partner until the moment I arrived.

Casey had been moved to the biggest room with the most equipment. She had torn underneath and lost lots of blood. From halfway down the bed, I could see the sheets drenched in red.

*That's my baby*, I thought, watching Casey. What Casey didn't realise was that she was in the exact room I'd lost Lewis nearly eighteen years earlier.

That panic and terror, of course, vanished the moment this new life – a healthy baby – was placed lovingly on Casey's chest and began to cry. As I watched Hali mewling in Casey's arms, I felt some of my own pain and trauma disappear, the room of nightmares turning into a happy place.

Casey was delivered via an emergency caesarean, and I woke up to find she had been born and taken from me. I gave birth naturally to Lewis, but he was swept away as people rushed to my side to intervene. Witnessing Hali arrive safe and sound felt like a balm. Being there was the honour of my life, and I'll never be able to thank Casey enough for letting me be part of it.

Hali and I have an unbelievable bond. I am *Nain* and Kings is *Taid* – Nana and Granddad in Welsh. These days, her personality is just coming out. When I go to the toilet, it takes me longer than Casey, and Hali notices. She stands outside the door, hands on her hips. '*NAIN!*' she shouts. 'Hurry *up!*' Casey says Hali talks about us at home, that she is besotted with Kings and me.

The feeling is reciprocated. She is the love of my life, and I truly believe she is the reason I am on this earth.

# CHAPTER SIXTEEN

# STOMA-FRIENDLY

Days after Wrexham made its debut in League Two, the club also achieved a significant milestone off the field: we made all of our accessible toilets stoma-friendly.

You don't have to do a lot at all to make facilities stoma-friendly. I didn't need to approach Ryan or Rob to sign-off a big chunk of the budget; I just had to clear it with the CEO and ask our maintenance man for a few hours of his time. It's one of the easiest ways that clubs can cater for people with hidden disabilities, but it's shocking that so many clubs just haven't followed suit. We unveiled our new facilities in our home game against MK Dons, whose ground Stadium MK is one of the few that is also stoma-friendly.

I liaised with Colostomy UK, a charity supporting people with a stoma, and they sent across a checklist. We needed a shelf so that ostomates (stoma users) could lay out their equipment on a sanitary surface – I'm very stringent with the club's cleaners about hygiene – and a mirror set at a particular height so that people can see their stomachs and stoma when changing. We needed hooks for wheelchair users and non-wheelchair users to hang their bags and coats out the way, and disposable bins, along with optional mats if people need to kneel to empty their stoma bag. The final touch was putting up #stomafriendly stickers from Colostomy UK on the toilet doors. That was all. These tiny things have an enormous impact on the people who need them, but they're so subtle that they go unnoticed by anyone else who uses those toilets.

Colostomy UK helped us break the news in a press release and put it best: 'Inadequate accessible toilet facilities act as a form of social exclusion. For people living with a stoma, a lack of suitable toilet facilities can be a huge barrier to doing many of the things most of us take for granted, like attending a football match.'

This project was close to my heart because I have two stomas. I have a colostomy bag, which takes waste from my bowel, and a urostomy bag, which collects urine. This has been the case since 2010, when I lost use of my bowels and bladder. I probably reacted more calmly to that than most people would because at the time it was just one of so many issues we were dealing with. Only five years earlier, I'd already been told that I wouldn't be able to walk and that I'd lost hearing in my right ear due to my cerebral bleed. Any of those things would be horrifying to someone confronted with just one, because they're life-defining – but relayed to me as they were, amid so many other things, they became smaller. I learned to deal with them quickly.

Would I have reacted the same way had I known it would involve twelve months bedbound – the most devastating, depressing and debilitating part of the whole thing?

The initial plan was an indwelling urinary catheter. A tube would be inserted into my bladder and the catheter would be held there by a water-filled balloon. The urine would collect in a bag strapped to the inside of my leg. The plan was to pass the balloon through the urethra and inflate it once it was inside me.

Within hours, we had a problem: my body was rejecting the balloon. Not only rejecting it but trying to expel it through the urethra. My body would spasm and spasm painfully until the balloon passed through me. Then we tried again. And again. And again. We tried over thirty times, day after day for over a month. Each time, we knew within hours that it had failed again when the spasms started. My body would push and push, and I would scream and scream, until I'd passed the inflated balloon.

The constant frustration was beaten out only by the relentless, excruciating pain. Since the bleed, I'd got used to readying myself for the worst-case scenario when it came to meeting with doctors and consultants, but that didn't make the meetings much easier. *Typical me*, I'd think. *This could only happen to us.*

The nurses agreed: most people with indwelling catheters don't have their bodies contorting in pain as they push them out. The consultant told us that it was like my body saw the balloon as a threat and wanted rid of it. Regularly, the nurses would tell me that they didn't know how I was coping with the pain.

After a few months, the consultant said the next step was a suprapubic catheter. They would cut a hole in my abdomen and directly into my bladder in what would be a forty-five-minute operation. The catheter would be attached to a collection bag strapped to my leg, which would need to be changed.

I was filled with trepidation. Having endured one failure, I did a lot of research. What I found wasn't reassuring: forums packed with patients listing issue after issue from their suprapubic catheters. They worked for some people, who talked about how they hoped to have them for life and had had no issues. Others had not been so lucky.

But the reality was that something had to be done. Choice didn't come into it. Did I want this surgery? I had to because I couldn't live life as I was. In a way, that lack of an alternative was a help. It wasn't a decision; it was a must.

As the general anaesthetic wore off, I began to fear something was amiss. Spasms raced across the right half of my abdomen to my bottom. I winced in pain as the spasms continued. The doctors told me that the area would take time to settle down after being disturbed for such a significant procedure, but as the days and weeks went on, the pain intensified to the point where I couldn't even sit up. My urology consultant even tried injecting Botox into my bladder to calm the spasms. Every three months, I returned as an outpatient for the procedure. The pain would subside, but the relief was so short-lived that it wasn't a long-term solution.

Literally moving from lying down to sitting up left me screaming in pain. The weight of my body on my backside would cause spasms because of the suprapubic catheter. The pain took my breath away. I felt winded, like I would pass out. It was beyond any kind of pain threshold, past what I could cope with. It was just off the scale.

I couldn't cope with being out of bed. In my adjustable bed, my legs were raised slightly – lying flat would put too much pressure on my stomach – and that was how I stayed for the next year.

Books, magazines, telly, consultant visits. Mostly, drifting in and out of sleep. Because I didn't have anything else to do. It sounds ridiculous, but I almost got institutionalised. Lying down was better than the alternative. For a weekly wash, I would be hoisted into my chair and through to the shower and I would scream the entire time. Only when I was lying down could I cope with the pain.

Kings and Casey carried on with life and found a new routine. Casey would say goodbye before she went to school, then when she came home, she'd come to me and sit on the bed. I would pull back the duvet and we'd snuggle in together to watch the soaps and chat, and later she'd have her tea with me. I couldn't play board games or cards with her because sitting up would be too painful. She talks fondly now of cuddling up together like that, and admits that she used to exaggerate some of the stories about her day and make them funnier and more fantastical because she thought I must have been bored all day and needed a good tale! All through the summer holidays, Kings took her on days out. They went to the zoo, to the beach, for walks. And at the end of every day, she'd sit on my bed and recount everything she'd done. She and Kings built a life that was communicated to me via pictures and videos.

Kings said that he would feel guilty for carrying on as normal while I watched on as an outsider. 'It's like we're telling you a story, instead of enjoying the time with you,' he said. But I knew that, once the front door shut behind him, he'd have to find a way to switch off. Casey needed a day out, and he needed a break.

I thought often of the trip to Disney World we had enjoyed shortly after our marriage, when Casey was only six. It was magical. Of course, it ended up being our last holiday together on a plane, so we never got the chance to return to America. It was a once-in-a-lifetime experience. I'm so glad Casey got to have that.

Through everything that's ever happened to me, my priority has been to keep Casey as grounded and as normal as we could. I kept thinking of the social workers: if we didn't give her a stable life, they'd say this wasn't a good environment for her. And I always felt like *I'd* lose Casey. Never Kings, but me.

Of course, she didn't have a normal childhood. She went from her mum being able to walk her to school to a life where her mum would just lay in bed. That was just what Mum did. Sometimes she'd become tearful: 'I really wish you could have come with us. I'm dead sad that you couldn't come.' But she had to accept it because there was no alternative. I would try to remind her that it wouldn't be forever, but, of course, that didn't totally banish her anxiety. She says that she doesn't remember many of the trips she went on that summer because she was thinking of me a lot.

She tried going to a group for young carers but said that she felt like a bit of a fraud there. As much as she knew that I was ill and had seen the impact that had on Kings and me, she felt like we had shielded her from a lot – so much so that she didn't feel like my carer. Casey told me that I reminded her of the four grandparents out of *Charlie and the Chocolate Factory*. That's a real reflection of how quickly, despite her fears, she adapted to the situation.

Just like after my bleed, I insisted that carers leave the door open for Casey. Hiding beneath baggy clothes and having my waste attached to me did feel degrading. While I might have felt some degree of shame, I was adamant that she never would. Happily, she would trot into the room while the carers tended to me, oblivious: 'Mum, Dad wants to know what you think of this. We're going to watch it on TV tonight.'

But one thing had changed by the time I'd had the suprapubic catheter fitted: my perspective. I was bedbound and in incredible pain, but I appreciated how lucky I was to even be alive. More than once, consultants told me that a lot of people wouldn't survive the kind of bleed I'd had. The bleed could have happened at any point in my life, and although I would have preferred it to have been when I was eighty, I thank God that I was thirty. I got married. I had a daughter. It could have happened to me as a teenager, and I'd have had none of that joy. In that way, I felt very blessed. That's the approach I've always had to take, even in bed, for twelve months, over a period that now feels like a blur.

One silver lining of that year was that, for the first time, I was able to get to know Matt as an adult. I had moved out when he was still really young, but by this point, he was travelling. We spoke every night and became close in a way we never had before.

After a year, my doctors recommended a Hartmann's procedure, a type of colectomy that removes part of the colon and makes a new opening through the abdomen (a colostomy). My bowels had never worked since the bleed and had no muscle tone, and I'd had to manually evacuate with a glove. My bladder didn't work, either, so I was advised that they needed to do a urostomy (an opening in the bladder) at the same time. This surgery would give me two stomas and I would leave with a bag for urine and a bag for faeces.

I had never heard of stoma surgery. Nobody had ever mentioned it before it was presented to me as the only option, and I was told in no uncertain terms that we had to act quickly. The plan had been to refer me to a bowel consultant, but there could be a wait of up to six months just to meet with them. In the end, I went to a private hospital in Wrexham for that consultation, whose staff agreed that a stoma was the way to go.

The surgery was scheduled for within the month. A bowel consultant and urology consultant would operate on me in tandem. I would be in surgery for eight hours. Afterwards, I was to go straight to intensive care. If there wasn't an intensive care bed available, I wouldn't be able to have the surgery.

This was the last resort. Unlike with the suprapubic catheter, I don't even remember thinking: *Do I want stoma surgery or not?* Maybe there was a choice, but after twelve months in bed and two catheters that hadn't worked, what choice was there, really? Stoma surgery it is – so when are we doing it?

Maybe we didn't ask the right questions, or enough of them. Then again, if you've never heard of a surgery, you don't know what to ask. But I feel now, looking back, that nothing was explained fully. I felt like a passenger.

I was absolutely terrified. This was huge surgery. The night before, my brother Ian came up to see me from Bexhill-on-Sea and I sobbed with him, petrified that I wouldn't make it through. 'What if I die in theatre?' I wept.

I hid my terror from Casey, adamant that she go to school as normal. The last thing we needed was her in a state over something she didn't understand. Naturally, Casey *was* upset and worried, in part because she didn't know what it all meant. 'When you're at school and eating your dinner and wondering what I'm doing,' I told her on the morning of the surgery, 'you've got to think: "My mum's having her bum stapled today!"'

That was how we made light of it. I always tried to explain things to her: this is who I am, and this is how we are dealing with things. Casey will say to me now that she can't believe some of the things I said to her, but humour was the best way for her – and anyone else – to understand it. On a night out, I'd say to my friends: 'You don't realise how lucky you are to be able to go to the toilet.'

On the operating table, surgeons would create a new opening on my stomach and staple inside my rectum so that faeces could no longer pass that way. Instead they would be diverted to the new opening on my stomach.

Horror hung over me even as I was wheeled into theatre. It was the most frightened I'd ever been in my life.

It wasn't much easier for Kings. For eight hours, he and Mum paced the hospital corridors. Ten minutes passed. Then another ten. And another. The stopwatch reached nine hours. Why had it over-run? Where was I? Another twenty minutes passed, then another thirty. By the time I'd been in surgery for ten hours, Kings and Mum were so frantic that the doctors let them into the recovery ward to see me. My blood pressure had dropped and I was shaking beneath piles of warm blankets, but I was full of relief when Kings and Mum burst into the deserted recovery room and saw for themselves that I'd survived.

When I arrived in ITU, I saw Anwen, a good friend who was also an advanced critical care practitioner there. She was in charge of my care that night and came to ask me whether I'd be comfortable with that, given we knew each other. The relief of having someone so familiar looking after me meant everything to me. I am incredibly grateful to her for being so reassuring at such a vulnerable time in my life, and I'll never forget the kindness she showed me.

After I was moved onto a general ward, a stoma nurse told me that she'd never seen anyone react so positively to the surgery because most patients just didn't want to deal with what had happened to them. For me, it was a relief: I was out of the intense pain that had kept me bedbound for a year. Perhaps it would have been different if I'd been younger, still going around town and looking for a partner, but I had my family and I knew I wasn't going to have any more children. I was just overwhelmed with hope that my life could begin again.

Kings didn't cope as well as I did. In the days after surgery, the stoma nurses show the patient how to change the bag for themselves. With one working hand, I wouldn't be able to. The nurses had made it clear to me from the beginning that I needed somebody to help me. They would have to teach Kings how to do it, how to clean the area, wipe the stoma and attach fresh bags.

'Right!' began Linda, the stoma nurse. 'We're going to look at how to change these!'

Kings stood at the foot of my bed in silence as she started to discuss what would be required. It was the first time he had seen my stomas: two bright red, fleshy, circular openings either side of my belly button. My large intestine, essentially.

'I can't do this.' He turned and silently left the room.

Linda went to the door and glanced down the ward. 'He's gone,' she said. 'What do we do now?'

'He'll be back,' I assured her. 'Just leave him to get his head around it.'

And he did, returning full of apologies later that night. He reflected that he was nervous and, he supposed, a bit squeamish. My being in a wheelchair had never bothered him, but he had never come across anyone with a stoma and didn't know what one would look like. He had imagined things, but his mind had probably tricked him into thinking he would react differently. Being confronted with the reality had briefly frightened him.

In the time he'd gathered himself, he'd accepted that this was our new reality. Walking out the room wouldn't mean anything was going to be different when he came back. He just needed space to get used to the idea, and by the time Linda came back the next day, he had. Now, we can get my bags changed in no time at all.

I still, though, have so many problems with my colostomy bag. Only as time has gone on have we realised, along with medical professionals, that the fact that half of my body was paralysed and very slow to transit was a bigger issue than we first understood. It didn't matter that they changed the opening from my bottom to my stomach if the bowel itself didn't work.

It's not just my colostomy bag: I also suffer daily problems with my bowel. In functioning bowels, mucus forms in the intestines to lubricate the colon. Every few weeks, I have contractions – akin to giving birth – as this mucus drips out of me. I have to wear pads until it ends, and that will be the case for the rest of my life. As I write this, I'm in the process of moving hospitals to see if some different doctors might be able to find some solutions to these kinds of issues I live with.

I'd been in theatre for so long on the day of the stoma surgery because there had been a complication with my bladder. The plan had been for the surgeons to leave my bladder in my body but bypass it – that, they said, would be safer than removing it completely. The consultant said after the surgery that he'd never seen a bladder in such a bad state, and he had had no choice but to take it out. He made the urostomy opening through my bowel instead.

'Unless you're in a life-or-death situation,' he warned, 'nobody should ever operate on your stomach again.'

. . .

On 8 August 2023, they told me I had two hours to live.

Days earlier, I'd welcomed Ryan and Hugh Jackman to the Quiet Zone. It had been the first game of the season. I'd joked that I was sharing my birthday with 10,000 fans and Hugh had given me a birthday kiss.

Then a routine meeting had ended in horrendous stomach cramps.

'I'll be all right,' I said, waving off my colleague's concerns. 'I'll be all right. I'll calm down.'

'No,' insisted Tina, who was then Wrexham's retail manager. 'I'm ringing Kings.'

By the time Kings came, the pain was at a different level and worsening by the second. I felt like my jeans were constricting me.

As soon as we got home, I burst into the bedroom and screamed at Kings in panic: 'I need to get undressed! They're getting tighter and tighter on my stomach!' My bowel problems mean that I'll often have cramps, but this was completely different.

This went on for hours, until I conceded that we needed to ring for an ambulance. The wait for one would be hours and I couldn't bear it any longer. Kings would have to take me.

In A&E, I screamed constantly, vomiting into a bowl. Still, people pointed and approached us: 'Oh! You're Kerry from Wrexham!' This happens all the time, but it's not ideal when you're so ill you can't talk to anybody.

'If you'd spent two more hours at home, you would be dead now,' said the consultant after I'd been stabilised. Unbeknownst to me, I'd had a hernia that had proceeded to strangulate my large intestine. Hernias, he told me, are common in people with stomas, but in most cases are formed by people bending or lifting – neither of which I'd done since the cerebral bleed. Silently, though, this hernia had grown and blocked the stoma. Despite the warnings of my stoma surgeon, we'd have to operate on my stomach again; there was no other choice.

I shivered in my hospital bed. *How had that happened?* I've always resisted going to hospital, scarred as I was by the hundreds of appointments that had brought bad news, so it took a lot for me to make that decision to call 999. The thought of what could have been had I been more stubborn was terrifying. Thankfully, they'd been able to stabilise me, but I would go under general anaesthetic in the morning to remove the hernia and remain in hospital for the next week. Even though I'd been told to never have stomach surgery again, without this procedure I'd have died.

Casey had recently given birth to our granddaughter Hali but had worked as a nurse for a couple of years. Even with a new baby at home, she came to the hospital and asked all the questions Kings and I wouldn't even think to ask.

The irony of it all was that I'd just featured in *Tidings*, the magazine produced by Colostomy UK, discussing all the work we'd done at Wrexham. Nurses were coming on shift and congratulating me for the article. 'Yes,' I'd say. 'We've just become stoma-friendly, and here I am, having nearly died because of my stoma.'

You couldn't write it.

'No one at this hospital has ever had flowers from Ryan Reynolds and Rob McElhenny,' said the receptionist, bringing into the room the largest bouquet of flowers I'd ever seen. 'Sadly, you're not allowed them on the ward. Someone will have to take them home.'

When I was finally discharged seven days later at 10 a.m., I was back working on my laptop in the afternoon – something that upset Rob when he learned about it later.

'No one knows my job like I do,' I told him. 'Fans need to be able to know what's going on.'

'You shouldn't have done that,' Rob said. 'You should have prioritised yourself.'

When I looked up from my emails, I saw their flowers, shrunken and shrivelled. Kings assured me that they had been magnificent and he had enjoyed them.

# EPILOGUE

## MAY 2025

I write this in the days after Wrexham's promotion to the Championship and another surreal week. Achieving three promotions in as many years, Wrexham have moved up the ladder at a speed none of us expected, with the players relishing their opportunity to make history. We knew that the takeover would change lives, but only by living it have we been able to appreciate just how drastically things have shifted for all of us. It has been beyond anything we could have dreamt of.

I have had a season ticket at the club for twelve years and I cannot remember a game that felt as good as the 3–0 win over Charlton that turned us into a Championship club.

Ryan flew back to LA the same weekend to walk a red carpet with Blake, and the club rolled out a red carpet of its own for player awards and staff celebrations. Afterwards, some players went to pack for their trip to Vegas the following week, while others came with the rest of the staff heading to the party.

We'd been told that every staff member could bring two guests. I knew who I needed to take. 'Mum,' I'd said, 'I'm awfully sorry, but I've only got two tickets. Dad has been on this football journey with me, so he has to be the one who comes.'

I wasn't sure whether a glitzy party would be his thing, but he had the night of his life. As the players came to talk to us, all I could focus on was Dad's face. He had his picture taken with Mickey Thomas, and I could see, in eyes that were struggling to take it all in, that he was so, so proud of me.

When I think about life in the Championship, all I can do is laugh. I was a volunteer in the National League less than five years ago – how has this happened? I am looking forward to the increased responsibility and a summer spent planning all the new initiatives I want to bring to the club, such as making Quiet Zone stewards more easily identifiable and offering them more specialist training.

I've also found my work on Wrexham's City of Culture board very rewarding. I was invited to apply in 2024 because of all of the work I'd done on disability and inclusion, and the club was hugely encouraging and enormously proud of me when, after three interviews, I was successful. That is the perfect example of my vision and the increased profile of the football club coming together to forge opportunities I never thought I'd be able to enjoy.

My great hope, though, is that disabled fans will be able to have the same experience they have at Wrexham at every ground they go to. The club now has a good reputation, and that's allowed me to have input with other clubs on a range of issues. A template for consistent, equal treatment, wherever fans are in the UK, would be the gold standard.

My other dream is that you, the reader, finish this book feeling inspired. Everyone is good at something – you just have to find out what your thing is. Some of us find those things as children; some of us need a bit longer. But we are all stronger than we think, and we all have something to offer. If you take one thing from my book, I hope that it's this.

I never thought that I would be the kind of person able to expose myself like this, sharing my story in all its raw, vulnerable detail. But I'm not ashamed of who I am or what I've been through, and I could never have completed this book without being true to myself. I couldn't leave out the most difficult parts, because that isn't how life works. Life is joy and pain, and every emotion between.

I used to wonder if there was any point in surviving everything I have been through. Doctors have said that it was a miracle I survived the bleed on my brain. After hearing that, I had to live life to the fullest. It wouldn't be fair to Kings and Casey if I didn't. And I love my life. I'm very proud of the life we have together. If I wasn't, I might as well have died at thirty. Every day, I think of how lucky I am to see and experience all that I do. I say often to Kings that I feel grateful for all my experiences because they have changed my perspective on life. So many people take it for granted, but I see every day as a gift.

At fifty, I look back and I can't get my head around how much has happened throughout my life. I had the most wonderful, close-knit family life growing up, with the best mum and dad a daughter could ever wish for, two amazing brothers, Ian and Matt, and Nan and Granddad. I was the richest kid going when it came to receiving their love and support, but even that couldn't change the adversity I faced. It might sound clichéd to say that those experiences made me stronger, but nothing could ring truer – hence the book's title. My family are my everything, from Kings, the kindest soul and most perfect life partner who changed my life forever, to Casey, who made true my dream of becoming a mum, to the beautiful little Hali, who made me a *nain*. The love and adoration I have for her blows my mind every day.

My story shows that if you keep going, you can prove everybody wrong – including yourself. You are not a prisoner of your past.

For Christmas last year, Kings and I bought Dad tickets for 'An Evening with Jeff Stelling', the legendary *Soccer Saturday* presenter. From the stage at William Aston Hall in Wrexham, he took questions from the audience and regaled us with tales of his famed broadcasting career. 'I know there will be a lot of Wrexham fans in here tonight,' he said, 'so I'm going to tell you a little story to prove I'm not bitter about your success.'

Hartlepool United FC, we all knew, was one of the other clubs that had been on Ryan and Rob's radar in the months before they decided to pick Wrexham. As Hartlepool's most famous fan, Stelling was invited onto a conference call with Rob, Ryan, Humphrey and Steve Horowitz, from the investment bank Inner Circle that helps to pair American investors with sports clubs.

'I got the phone call from Hollywood,' Stelling said. 'I was the one who told them all about Hartlepool. You might have got Ryan Reynolds and Rob McElhenney, but I got the call from them. No one else in this room can say that.'

I turned to my dad and whispered in his ear: 'I can.'

# AFTERWORD
## BY ROB McELHENNEY

So here we are. The end of the book. The back of the room. The credits rolling. And if you're anything like me – if you've made it this far – you're probably wondering: *Wait, didn't Ryan Reynolds already say everything there is to say about Kerry Evans?* But even before that, I imagine some of you are thinking: *Hang on. Why are we hearing from Rob in the first place? Why would I listen to him about Kerry? I just spent a whole book hearing from Kerry herself – what does this guy know that she didn't already say?*

Fair question.

I mean, Kerry's the one who lived it. She's the one who faced down challenges most of us can't even imagine – again and again – and somehow found a way to help others in the process. She's the one who's been on the front lines, fighting for people who needed her, long before any of us showed up with cameras and good intentions.

So yeah. Why would you listen to me?

Well, for one thing, I'm a pretty good storyteller. Not as good as Ryan, obviously – his foreword made me want to laugh, cry and buy maple syrup in bulk. But I've spent the better part of my life figuring out how to make people feel something. And when I say that Kerry

Evans makes you feel something, I mean it. She makes you feel the beautiful weight of what it means to *belong*. She makes you feel the quiet, everyday courage it takes to make space for people who've been pushed to the edges. And she makes you feel – really feel – the responsibility to carry some of that weight yourself.

Also – let's be honest – I'm here because I'm in a bit of a word-war with Ryan, and I'll be damned if I let him have the last word. That's why I agreed to do the AFTERword. Honestly, this might be the first time in the history of memoirs where the foreword and afterword are written by two guys openly trying to out-sentiment each other. And if that's the case? Good. Because Kerry Evans deserves a whole book *so full* of love and admiration it spills out of the binding and into your lap.

Now, I know you've just read her story. You've seen the pain, the triumphs, the setbacks, the victories and the moments that don't fit neatly into a sports docuseries highlight reel. You've read about the woman who literally transformed trauma into action. Who, after life threw every kind of obstacle in her way, didn't just keep going – she *changed the game* for people who'd been left out for too long.

But let me tell you what Kerry means to *me*.

When Ryan and I first started this wild Wrexham adventure, we thought we were buying a football club. Turns out, we were buying a front-row seat to a masterclass on what it means to *care*. And Kerry Evans? She's the teacher.

I'll never forget one of the first times I saw her – this whirlwind of purpose, gliding around with her phone buzzing, a thousand little emergencies landing at her feet like pigeons in a park. She'd handle one, then the next and the next, always with that same quiet determination, that 'I'll get it done' energy that makes you believe in the possibility of impossible things.

And here's the thing. Kerry doesn't do it for the spotlight. She doesn't do it for a paycheque (though God knows she deserves the biggest one the club can give). She does it because she knows – *deeply* knows – that for some people, coming to a football match is the highlight of their week. And if they can't get in the building because of a step, policy or thoughtless design, that's not just an inconvenience; that's a heartbreak.

Kerry refuses to let that happen.

She's the reason a grandfather in a wheelchair doesn't miss his grandson's first match – because nothing should stand in the way of that memory. She's the reason a teenage girl with autism feels safe enough to lift her voice and sing with the crowd – because she's not an outsider here, she's part of the chorus.

Kerry's the reason no one feels like they're on the outside looking in. They're not 'others'; they are Wrexham.

She's the heart beating beneath the chants, the quiet voice behind the roar of the crowd. She's the person who reminds us – me, Ryan, the entire club – why we're doing this in the first place. It's not just about football. It's about community. It's about belonging. It's about making damn sure no one gets left behind.

And I'll be honest: I didn't know that at first. I thought it. I hoped for it. But I didn't *know* it. When I first walked into the Racecourse, I thought: *Cool. We're here to make a football documentary. This is going to be fun!* What I didn't realise is that we were stepping into a place where people like Kerry had been fighting, day in and day out, to make life just a little bit easier for people who don't always get a break in life.

Let me tell you a little secret: Kerry doesn't just make it look easy. It *isn't* easy. It's messy. It's complicated. It's exhausting. There are days she's had to push through pain most of us can't imagine. There are days she's questioned whether she's making a difference at all. But here's the thing about Kerry: she *keeps showing up*. And in doing so, she shows the rest of us how to do the same.

Ryan said it best – this isn't just a story of inspiration. It's *ignition*. It's the spark that lights a fire inside you. And if you're reading this and thinking, *What can I do?* – that's it. Show up. Care. Make a little room for someone else.

Because that's what Kerry's done. For years. For decades. For *this* club. For *these* people.

Kerry Evans is a once-in-a-generation person. She's the reason Wrexham feels like home – not just to the people who were born there but to all of us who've been lucky enough to find our way into this story.

So, Ryan, if you're reading this, I see your foreword, and I raise you this afterword.

Kerry, thank you for letting us tell your story. Thank you for *living* your story, for fighting the hard fights, for loving this club and its people with a ferocity that humbles the rest of us. And thank you for *sharing* your story so that even those who know you well can get a closer look at what keeps a lionheart beating.

To everyone reading this: let's make sure Kerry's story doesn't just end here. Let's carry it forward. Let's keep the door open. Let's keep showing up.

With love, admiration, and a competitive spirit that I *hope* is just enough to one-up Ryan's foreword,

*Rob Mac*
*Wrexham AFC, Co-Owner*
*Licensed Blanket Folder*
*Forever Grateful*

# ACKNOWLEDGEMENTS

To get the opportunity to write a book has been beyond my wildest dreams. Since starting my role as disability liaison officer at Wrexham AFC, it's always been, for me, about making a difference. My desire for this project has always been to inspire others. If one reader feels they too could follow a dream and make it into a reality, the sole purpose of this book will have been achieved.

My journey so far has involved the support of many people, and I would like to thank them all.

Katie Whyatt, your hard work and dedication to this book, to helping me tell my story over the past twelve plus months, has been incredible. You're such a talented writer, and I wouldn't have wanted to do this book with anyone else. I will forever be grateful.

David Luxton, my agent, for believing in my story, and for pairing me with Katie, the perfect partner. I will always be eternally grateful for the support and guidance on this journey.

Biteback Publishing, for giving me this wonderful opportunity and being a huge support throughout the whole process.

Mum and Dad, who I love unconditionally. Without their unwavering support throughout my life, life would have been beyond impossible. My parents never accepted that I wouldn't ever be able to achieve, and although I doubted myself on numerous occasions, they never doubted me. I cannot thank them enough. You have made me into the person I am today and I will be forever grateful. Love you both always.

Nan and Granddad, if there was ever a grandchild going to write a book and dedicate it to you, I'm sure I'd be the last to come to mind. You both meant the world to me. You were my everything! I was at the front of the queue when they were giving out the best grandparents. You were simply the best. The close relationship we had was incredibly special and if I can be half as good a grandparent to Hali, I will be beyond proud. Love you both, and miss you.

Joanne, what can I say? You have literally been my saviour in life. My true best friend, the person who at times in my life was my only friend in the whole world. Our friendship has already spanned forty-four years, and I hope it will last a lifetime. I will love you forever and beyond, and I look forward to growing old together.

Kings, my special friend who then became my everything and my amazing husband. You make my life complete. I can never put into words what our life together means to me. You saved me, became my rock and made me a far better person. You have inspired me and given me the confidence to believe in myself again. No one has ever made me feel as special as you do on a daily basis. In a million lifetimes, I'd pick you every time. You simply complete me. I love you beyond words.

Casey, my beautiful daughter. You're the most precious girl on the planet. You make me prouder every day. Being your mum has been the biggest honour of my life and my proudest achievement to date. I love you always, sweetheart. You are the most amazing mummy to Hali, and your career choice shows the caring girl you are. I will always love you more.

Rhys, if I can do this, then so can you. You must follow your dreams and keep believing. Thank you for taking such good care of my girl and being the most amazing daddy to Hali. I love you loads.

Hali, the light of my life. Becoming your *Nain* has to be the most special moment ever. Being at your birth was incredibly moving and emotional and, although you are only two, I can already tell that the bond we have will never be broken. You make every day brighter, and I will love you unconditionally forever, baby girl.

Ian and Matt, who have forever been there for me. I couldn't have wished for better brothers. I bet you never thought you'd have a sister you could chat all things football with! Thanks for everything. I really do appreciate and love you both loads. Thank you also to my sisters-in-law Lizzii and Holly, and my beautiful niece who I treasure, Ellis.

The Robertses – Auntie Carol, Uncle Glyn, Mark and Paul and your family. I have loved all the holidays and special times we spend together.

The Joneses – Uncle Del, Richard, Lyndsey, Anthony, Codie and Lucy and all your extended family. Special thanks to Lucy for always keeping my nails so beautiful.

Auntie Gwyn and Uncle Glyn Davies in Canada, and their families who I have taken to my heart.

The Evans family, and my amazing mother-in-law, Barbara, who I adored. Thank you for welcoming me into your hearts, Davina and Chris, Nathan and Mel, my nephews Barney and Daniel, my niece Lowri and your families.

Phil and Irena, thank you for welcoming me into your family.

Gric, thanks for being you, and for loving and supporting me all these years.

Mrs Hartlepayne, thank you for taking me under your wing; your support meant the world to me and I will always be grateful.

'Our' Dave Lindop, thank you for giving me my first ever job. I loved working for you and appreciated your kindness.

Ian Herbert, for the huge support you have been throughout this book process. I really value your friendship.

Everyone at Wrexham AFC: the WST Trust Board, for initially believing in me and giving me my voluntary opportunity; managers, players, CEOs and staff, for always treating me as you have. I have never felt disabled among you all. You have made me feel like an equal. This chapter in my life has been incredibly powerful, and every single one of you has made my job at Wrexham so enjoyable.

The Wrexham fans, thank you from the bottom of my heart for believing in me and giving me the most outstanding support throughout.

Everyone in my incredibly special Quiet Zone, you make my job so worthwhile, and I will forever be grateful for all your support.

Not forgetting Ryan Reynolds and Rob McElhenny. You will never realise how much your belief in me has changed my life. It is a true honour to work at your beloved Wrexham AFC, and I will be eternally grateful for the opportunity you gave me. I promise to give you 110 per cent, always.

Thayer Joyce from More Better, for the huge support you have been throughout on this journey. I really have appreciated your input.

Humphrey Ker, for being the nicest person I could ever wish to meet, a huge support to me through my role and for encouraging me to write this book. You were the first person I ever mentioned it to at the club.

Owain Davies, I'd be lost without the unwavering guidance, support from you and all the outstanding staff at Level Playing Field.

Spencer Harris and Colin Williams, how can I ever thank you both? You gave me an opportunity that I grabbed with both hands. I am truly honoured to now call you both friends.

Phil Bennett, my first ever boss at Wrexham AFC. You were so good with me and inspired me to be better. There were a few times you talked me out of walking away in the early days, when I was struggling. I will be forever grateful for that.

Julie Greenwood, for being the person who I look up to, and for always listening and helping guide me. I look forward to the next chapter with you! Thank you for everything.

Wayne from the 'world famous' Turf, thank you for coming on this mad journey with me and always supporting me.

Kerry Roberts from the Wrexham Branch of the National Autistic Society. Without your friendship and backing, I couldn't have achieved what we have at Wrexham AFC. I will always be grateful.

Macron Sports Wrexham, for the huge support you have shown me. Special mention to Andy and Wendy.

Andy from Macclesfield FC, you truly are the reason this journey began, and I will forever hold you in my heart. Thank you.

Peter Schriewersmann at Hotel Wrexham, for being an incredible support and believing in my role and also for hosting the book launch. I consider you a great friend.

Justine and Allan, Nicky and Jason, our friendship means the world to Kings and me. Thank you for all the support and being such extraordinary friends in my life.

To all these special people who have either contributed with photos, stories, letters or emails to this book: Mike of White and Williams, Matt from Barlows, Castle Mews Carpets, Jeff Brazier, Rob Stead for my cover photos, Steve Webster, Colin Henrys, Akil Wright, Kevin and Debbie Vaughan, Ann Burden, Mike Smith, Helen Docking, Alison Tipping, Ian Heard Jones, Karen Griffiths, DJ Povey, Amy Davies, Nicky Cunningham, Simon Milton, Ben Tozer, James McLean, the one and only super Paul Mullin, Peter Wynne, Catherine Williams, Sian Davies, Geoff Scott and Mr Wrexham – Geraint Parry.

Valentine Travel Solutions, W. B. Environmental Ltd., Richard Watkin from the Fat Boar and more recently Wrexham & Prestige Taxis, our sponsors for our wheelchair-accessible away travel – you all made this service a reality, so thank you.

FX Productions' film crew, especially Paddy and Milos. Thanks for your incredible patience with me and for showcasing my work at Wrexham AFC so beautifully.

To every single person who has been an inspiration within my life, far too many to mention – thank you all.

And, finally, to every single person who has read this book. I hope I leave you with some inspiration to follow your dreams.